P9-DJL-075

TOGETHER

Discover the inspiring partnership that formed more than a century after the Supreme Court's infamous "separate-but-equal" decision.

Keith Plessy and Phoebe Ferguson were both born in New Orleans in 1957. Sixty-five years earlier, in 1892, a member of each of their families met in a Louisiana courtroom when Judge John Howard Ferguson found Homer Plessy guilty of breaking the law by sitting in a train car for white passengers. The case of *Plessy v. Ferguson* went all the way to the U.S. Supreme Court, which ruled that "separate-but-equal" was constitutional, sparking decades of unjust laws and discriminatory attitudes.

In *Together*, Amy Nathan threads the personal stories of Keith Plessy and Phoebe Ferguson into the larger history of the *Plessy v. Ferguson* case, race relations, and civil rights movements in New Orleans and throughout the U.S. She tells the inspiring tale of how Keith and Phoebe came together to change the ending of the story that links their families in history. It's "a flip on the script," said Keith.

> *"Some of the things I loved about* Together *are its connections of critical big historic moments to individual personal understandings; its readable summary of Reconstruction; and its theme of 'inspiring others,' both the whole concept of descendants coming together to make change, and the way readers can see specific examples of what has been and can be done."*
>
> —Dr. Mary Battenfeld, American and New England Studies, Boston University

TOGETHER

AN INSPIRING RESPONSE TO THE
"SEPARATE-BUT-EQUAL" SUPREME COURT DECISION
THAT DIVIDED AMERICA

Amy Nathan

PAUL DRY BOOKS
Philadelphia 2021

PASADENA LIBRARY, CENTRAL
1201 Jeff Ginn Memorial Drive
Pasadena, TX 77506-4895

Cover Art: A panel from Ayo Scott's mural "'These Are Times':
The Legacy of Homer Plessy," which is located in Plessy Park in
New Orleans, Louisiana, commissioned by the NOCCA Institute.
© Ayo Scott / http://ayoscott.com

In his website description of this section of the mural, the artist
poses a question: ". . . what might liberty and justice look like
through the eyes of another person."

First Paul Dry Books Edition, 2021

Paul Dry Books, Inc.
Philadelphia, Pennsylvania
www.pauldrybooks.com

Copyright © 2021 Amy Nathan

All rights reserved.

Printed in the United States of America

Library of Congress Control Number: 202094529

For Keith Plessy and Phoebe Ferguson

CONTENTS

TOGETHER

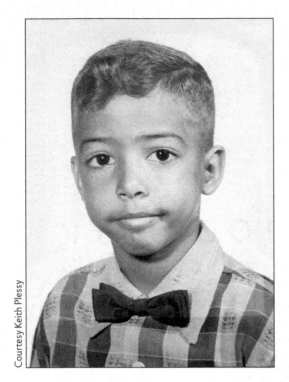

Courtesy Keith Plessy

*Keith Plessy
and Phoebe Ferguson,
about seven years old.*

Courtesy Phoebe Ferguson

RULED OUT

"Like all the boys in my neighborhood, I liked to play football and baseball in local parks," said Keith Plessy, who grew up in New Orleans in the 1950s and '60s. "The closest park in walking distance from my house had space for two baseball fields, and room for a football field between the baseball fields. It featured a swimming pool in the summer, too. But I was never allowed to play there as a child on Saturdays and Sundays. The park had a rule: Only white kids could play there on weekends."

Keith and other children of color could stand outside the fence and watch the white kids play. "But we couldn't go in. On days when we had the park, the white kids couldn't come into the park, either. There wasn't a sign with that rule. It was just understood that white kids had the park all day every weekend. We had to squeeze in our playing after school, before it got dark," explained Keith.

"As a child, I was always questioning things when it came to the color of a person's skin—why people who were considered to be 'white' got better treatment than others. I lived in a multi-racial neighborhood," he noted. "There were African Americans, Irish Americans, Jewish Americans, Italian Americans, and Native Americans. Sometimes it was hard to tell whether people were Black or white. I've been called Puerto Rican several times. On some streets people got along like we

St. Roch Park, where Keith played as a child.

Courtesy Wes Michaels, Spackman Mossop Michaels

were family." But in other areas, some boys might beat him up. "It wasn't discussed much at home or at school."

Figuring out where he could and couldn't go in his neighborhood wasn't easy. "There were restaurants that wouldn't let Black people come inside to eat. We had to go around to the back door and order food to take out." Some white shopkeepers were nice, but others weren't. "At one bakery shop, the lady behind the counter kept skipping me. Any white customer that came in, she would say, 'Oh, what do you need?' But it was like I wasn't there." So Keith took the ice cream sandwich he wanted to buy and walked out of the store. *Then* the shopkeeper noticed him—and almost had him arrested. The police called his mother to come get him.

"I got a good spanking when I got home. My mother said, 'That's not what we do. We don't steal.' But I told her, 'They kept skipping me.' So my mother told me, 'Next time, put it down, and don't go to that store again. Go places where you

Courtesy Keith Plessy

Keith's parents, Marie Verna Mae Blanchard Plessy and Paul Gustave Plessy.

won't be treated that way. Don't let anyone take your sunshine away from you.'"

He loved his elementary school, but it got its start in the early 1900s because of another situation that didn't make sense to Keith as a child. The African American community had to create this school on its own because the city refused to provide an elementary school for children of color in Keith's neighborhood. Even years later, in the early 1960s, when Keith was ready to start elementary school, he and many other children of color still weren't allowed to attend the city's schools for white children. "It puzzled me a lot why there were these rules," said Keith.

Confusing rules about skin color puzzled Phoebe Ferguson as a child, too. The same age as Keith, she lived in a different New Orleans neighborhood and went to a private elementary school that only white students attended. She had a babysitter that she loved, Minnie Lou Williams, who had helped take care of her since Phoebe was six months old. "We did a lot of fun things together," Phoebe recalled. "We played together in the backyard, or went to nearby playgrounds to swing. We played 'Go Fish' a lot. Minnie took me trick-or-treating, too."

Courtesy Phoebe Ferguson

Photo © Alan Karchmer

Left: *Minnie Lou Williams, the babysitter who took care of Phoebe as a child, in a photo from the 1980s.*

Above: *The carousel at City Park in New Orleans.*

However, one day an unfair rule ruined a fun afternoon with Minnie. "When I was about six years old, I remember going to a movie theater with Minnie," said Phoebe. "The man at the theater told Minnie that I could sit downstairs at the movie, but Minnie had to sit upstairs. What did that mean? It was very confusing. I certainly wasn't going to go to the movies without her or sit in another place. We walked home in total silence, holding hands. I remember feeling really sad and not understanding."

That's how Phoebe found out that many movie theaters at the time let only white people sit downstairs. Black people had to sit upstairs in the balcony. "It didn't make sense to me. I felt that the man who said that was mean." Another day, Minnie

Courtesy Phoebe Ferguson

Phoebe's parents,
Anne Williams Ferguson
and William Loring Ferguson, Jr.

took Phoebe to the city's amusement park. Phoebe could sit on a horse on the park's carousel, but Minnie wasn't allowed to ride with her. The carousel was only for white people.

Phoebe doesn't remember whether when she was a child she spoke with her mother about what had happened at the movie theater and the amusement park. She knows now that if she had spoken up, her mother would have said what happened was very wrong. Phoebe learned later that her mother had been volunteering with groups that tried to put an end to the idea of separating people by race. But Phoebe didn't know that when she was little. To young Phoebe, those movie theater and carousel rules were "definitely confusing and not fair."

Also puzzling were the differences she saw between her house and the home of Minnie's aunt, Georgia Lee Kearny, who worked as a housekeeper for Phoebe's family. "I hung around Georgia a lot. I remember when I found out that she had to take three buses to get to our house. When I was older, around eight or nine, I went to her house and saw that after she finished working with us, she still had to go home and cook and clean for her family. I remember being deeply affected by the sacrifices Georgia was making in order to work for our family. I don't know why I went over there. I was try-

Courtesy Phoebe Ferguson

Georgia Lee Kearny, in a photo with Phoebe from the 1980s.

ing to make sense of the disparity between our living situations. I was also getting to know who she was outside of my house. Not that I needed to know anything more about her in terms of her integrity or her ability to give love to children that were not hers. But to see her interaction with her family and see that there were multiple relatives, nieces, nephews, and cousins that depended on her cooking for them as well. That affected me a lot."

Both Phoebe Ferguson and Keith Plessy were born in New Orleans in 1957, but they never met while they were children. Phoebe's father died when she was ten, and then she and her mother moved to California. Years later, Keith and Phoebe met when they were adults, with children of their own. By then, they had both learned something amazing: Sixty-five years before Keith and Phoebe were born, a member of each of their families had also met.

That meeting took place on October 13, 1892, when Phoebe's great-great-grandfather was in a New Orleans courtroom with a cousin of Keith's great-grandfather. Their being together in that courtroom had a lot to do with why there were rules and laws that kept Black and white people apart.

By the time Keith and Phoebe met as adults, they were both ready to create a new ending for the story that links their two families forever.

© The NOCCA Institute, Elizabeth McMillan photo, New Orleans Center for Creative Arts Drama Department production of Se-Pa-Rate

*There are no photos of Homer Plessy, the cousin of Keith Plessy's
great-grandfather who met Phoebe Ferguson's great-great-grandfather
in 1892. But in 2010, New Orleans high school student Timothy
Bellows, Jr., portrayed Homer Plessy in a play called Se-Pa-Rate. He
was part of a group of high school students who created the play
themselves to explore the connections between their own lives and
what Homer Plessy did. (More about the play later in this book.)*

KEITH PLESSY'S
LONG-AGO RELATIVE

Keith Plessy's relative who met Phoebe Ferguson's relative all those years ago was Homer Plessy. He was a twenty-nine-year-old African American shoemaker and school reform activist who lived in New Orleans. Rules and laws that kept Black and white people apart troubled him, just as they would trouble Keith and Phoebe many years later.

Homer Plessy found an unusual way to protest against an especially unjust law that Louisiana's legislature passed in 1890, the Separate Car Act. This new law required that Black and white passengers stop doing what they had been doing for more than twenty years, ever since Homer Plessy was five years old—sitting together in the same cars on a train. Instead, they would have to sit in separate cars. Some cars would only be for white riders. Other cars would only be for Black passengers.

This new law outraged Homer Plessy and other people of color in New Orleans because it didn't treat them as full American citizens, with the same rights as white citizens. People of color in Louisiana and other southern states had only gained equal rights about twenty-five years earlier, when the Civil War ended. They didn't want to lose any of those newly-won rights.

Courtesy Louisiana Division/City Archives, New Orleans Public Library

Rodolphe Desdunes.

As far as we know, Homer Plessy didn't keep a diary or write to others about the Separate Car Act. But he probably supported the views of Rodolphe Desdunes, a writer for *The Crusader*, a Black-owned New Orleans newspaper. He wrote an article in the newspaper on July 4, 1891, a patriotic day celebrating one of the ideals the United States was founded on: that all men are created equal. In this article, Desdunes said the following about the new Separate Car Act:

Among the many schemes devised by the Southern statesmen to divide the races, none is so insulting as the one which provides separate cars for black and white people . . . It is like a slap in the face of every member of the black race . . . We are American citizens and it is our duty to defend our constitutional rights.

To understand why Homer Plessy, Rodolphe Desdunes, and other *Crusader* readers felt compelled to protest against this new law, it helps to look at what things were like for people of color in New Orleans in the years leading up to the law's creation. It's a roller coaster ride of a story, starting with a painful period of few rights at all, followed by a brief upswing with new rights won, leading to a downward spiral as rights began to be snatched away.

Rights Denied

Before the Civil War, people of color in New Orleans had few rights, even though in 1850, about ten years before the start of the war, they made up nearly a quarter of the city's 116,000 residents.

The largest group of people of color in New Orleans were enslaved. Many had to work as household servants for slaveholders. Others were sent to work for their enslavers in brickyards or on the riverfront docks of this Mississippi River city. Other enslaved people lived on nearby plantations where they were forced to harvest sugar cane, cotton crops, and do other work. In some sugar cane-growing areas, there were more Black people than white people. Harvesting and processing sugar cane was backbreaking and dangerous work, particularly the grinding and boiling of sugar cane stalks to turn them into sugar that could be sold. For several months after harvest time, enslaved workers had to do the grinding and boiling work round the clock. Exhaustion could lead to severe injuries from the open furnaces and the rollers used in the grinding.

Enslaved laborers had no rights at all. They were not allowed to vote or learn to read. Those who tried to learn to read faced serious punishment, as did the people who taught them. Yet, ever since the arrival of the first slave ships in Louisiana in 1719, it was the labor and farming know-how of the enslaved that made Louisiana prosperous. The first African captives were forced to work for French settlers who had been failing on their own at farming in this new land. Slave labor continued to power Louisiana's progress up to the end of the Civil War—for more than 140 years.

Before the Civil War, free people of color also lived in New Orleans. In 1850, they made up just under ten percent of the city's population. Records show more than twice as many free people of color had lived in the city twenty years earlier. White officials kept placing new restrictions on these free people, which may have caused some to move to other, more welcoming parts of the U.S. or to other countries. Those of mixed race with fair complexions may have tried to "pass" as white and so would no longer choose to identify themselves as people of color to officials collecting information on the city's population.

Homer Plessy's parents and grandparents were members of the city's community of free people of color. Homer was born in New Orleans midway through the Civil War on March 17, 1863. This was a little over two months after President Abraham Lincoln issued the Emancipation Proclamation that announced an end to slavery. Homer Plessy had no first-hand

Courtesy Keith Plessy

JOSEPH GUSTAVE PLESSY BORN 1850/JAN. 30 HOMER A. PLESSY'S FIRST COUSIN

KEITH M. PLESSY 2003

Keith Plessy's cousin Geraldine Talton had a photo of Keith's great-grandfather, Joseph Gustave Plessy, who was Homer Plessy's cousin. In 2003, Keith used that photo to make this drawing. When Hurricane Katrina hit New Orleans in 2005, Talton's house was engulfed with water. "She lost everything," said Keith, including the original photo of his great-grandfather.

memory of slavery, but he would have heard stories about what the city had been like for people of color before the war. Soon he would have his own experiences of unfair treatment in the city of his birth.

Some free people of color came to New Orleans before the Civil War as free men and women. Others had once been enslaved. They may have been freed by their enslavers, who in many cases were actually their fathers. Or they may have managed to buy their own freedom. Some slaveholders paid enslaved people fifty cents if they had to work on a Sunday or do extra work for the slaver or for others.

Sometimes the money to buy a person's freedom came from another individual. This happened to Homer Plessy's great-grandmother, Agnes Ramis. Her family had been enslaved ever since her own great-grandmother was captured in Africa in the early 1700s and forcibly transported on one of the slave ships that brought thousands of African captives to Louisiana, which at that time was a colony of France. In 1779, Agnes, then twenty years old, gained her freedom when Mathieu Devaux, a forty-two-year-old white Frenchman living in Louisiana, provided the money to pay Agnes's white slaveholder. Agnes and Mathieu would later have seven children. Marriage between white people and people of color was illegal and remained so until after the Civil War, but officially unrecognized relationships like theirs still occurred.

The land that is now the state of Louisiana had been part of a huge French colony in North America for nearly a hundred years. That colony stretched from what is now New Orleans up the middle of the continent to Canada. In 1682, a French explorer named all that territory for France's King Louis XIV and claimed it for France. Before the Civil War, many who lived in what is now the state of Louisiana were of mixed-race, had French relatives, and spoke French, as the Plessy family did. Luckily for Homer Plessy's great-grandmother, Agnes Ramis, Spain took control of Louisiana in 1769, ten years before she won her freedom. Spain's laws made it a little easier for enslaved people to seek their freedom than it had been under French control, or than it would be from 1803 on, when the U.S. bought from France the territory that includes today's state of Louisiana. It became a U.S. state in 1812.

WORDS MATTER

Terms used to identify Americans of African ancestry have changed over the years. "Negro" was used in the 19th and early 20th centuries, as was "colored." Both fell out of favor in the 1960s and the 1980s, replaced by "Black" and "African American," which are used in this book except for quoted passages from earlier times when those older terms were in use. "People of color," also used in this book, has Louisiana roots. Louisiana's Civil Code of 1808 required free Black people to write next to their names on documents the initials "f.p.c.," for "free person of color" (or "f.m.c." and "f.w.c.," for free man or woman of color). They began referring to themselves that way, too. In addition, mixed-race people of color who were born in Louisiana, enslaved or free, also called themselves Creoles. Many had French ancestry, but others with different ancestry also identified as Creole, as have some white people. "Enslaved" is another term that is frequently used now. It serves as a reminder that those who in earlier times were referred to as "slaves" were individuals with hopes and dreams who had been forced into an unjust situation that denied them all rights.

As a free woman of color, Agnes owned property in New Orleans. She also bought and sold enslaved people, as some free people of color did. A document found by one of Keith Plessy's cousins, Michael Nolden Henderson, suggests that Agnes may have engaged in the slave trade in order to free people, including buying and freeing her own mother.

Before the Civil War, free people of color in New Orleans had the right to hold jobs, own property, and run businesses. Some became successful merchants, real estate brokers, doctors, artists, and writers. Others worked as carpenters, as Homer Plessy's father did, or as shoemakers, iron workers, furniture makers, and other craftsmen. For women, working as a seamstress was a possibility, as was buying and selling property. Some free people of color owned plantations and were slaveholders.

But no matter how successful they were, free people of

color were not allowed to vote. They could not testify in court against white people. They could not send their children to the city's public schools, even though they had to pay taxes which helped fund the public schools that white youngsters attended.

Free people of color were also not allowed to sit with white people, whether in streetcars, restaurants, or theaters, nor were they allowed to be treated in the same part of a hospital as white people. Black Codes, written by white officials, set rules for how all Black people—free or enslaved—had to behave, such as never acting as if they were equal to white people.

After the U.S. took control of Louisiana and it became a state, white slaveholders controlled the state's government. White legislators passed laws that tried to limit the number of free people of color who could enter the state. New laws also required that free people of color register with the state government. Officials feared that a large population of free people of color might encourage the enslaved to seek their freedom. This was a big worry for New Orleans slaveholders, because for the first thirty years that Louisiana was a state, there were more people of color in New Orleans than white people.

Despite the lack of public schools, many free people of color managed to receive a good education if their families could afford the tuition fees at the few private or religious

WAR OF THE PEWS

An exception to the city's social separation by skin color was St. Augustine's, a Catholic church established in 1841 at the request of free people of color in New Orleans. Some white people were upset that a church was being built for the Black community and tried to buy up most of the pews. (At that time churches charged fees for the right to sit in certain pews.) But free people of color bought many more pews than white parishioners did, and they bought pews for enslaved people to use as well. This church, which Homer Plessy later attended, was for many years the country's most integrated congregation.

schools that allowed their children to attend. Other families sent their youngsters to other cities, or to France, to attend school. In 1848, a new private school for free children of color opened. It charged no tuition for orphans and only a small fee for others. The money to start this school came from a free woman of color, Marie Couvent. She stated in her will that after her death she wanted her money to be used to create such a school. She had become wealthy buying property, building houses, and renting them to other free people of color. She was also a slaveholder. She couldn't read but wanted others to be able to do so.

This school provided an excellent education for more than two hundred girls and boys a year. Rodolphe Desdunes, the newspaper writer, served on the school's board, as did other prominent members of the free Black community. Some also taught at the school. Many of the school's supporters, teachers, and students later played roles in winning equal rights for

Courtesy Louisiana Division/City Archives, New Orleans Public Library

In the book he wrote about Creole history, Rodolphe Desdunes included this photo of Victoria Lecène, the winner of an award as a Couvent School student.

people of color. However, four years after the Couvent school opened, a new law gave police officers the right to search schools like this to see if any enslaved children were among the students. In fact, some free people of color did secretly teach enslaved students and had to move those classes often to keep a step ahead of the police.

White officials placed limits on Black education because they feared that educated enslaved people would revolt. Without enslaved laborers to harvest the state's sugar cane and cotton crops, Louisiana would never have become one of the richest states in the nation, as it was just before the Civil War.

Plantation owners weren't the only ones whose wealth depended on slavery. Others in New Orleans had a financial interest in a new kind of slave market that arose after 1808, when the U.S. stopped participating in the international slave trade. Slave ships no longer brought people captured in Africa or other countries to serve as slaves in the U.S. But slavery still continued. Plantation owners wanted additional enslaved laborers, especially in the Deep South, where cotton and sugar cane production was booming. To meet those needs, the domestic slave trade began.

Slaveholders in the upper South made money by selling some of their enslaved people to slave markets farther south. Family members were often sold individually. That tore families apart. New Orleans became the capital of the new domestic slave trade. It had the largest slave markets in the country, using pens to hold the many individuals to be sold. Local dealers, lawyers, and other business people in the city made money handling the details involved in the buying and selling of human beings.

All those in New Orleans who benefitted financially from slavery had a keen interest in trying to prevent slave revolts. They knew rebellions were possible. Some revolts had even happened in the early 1700s on the ships that transported the first enslaved captives from Africa to Louisiana. In 1729, an uprising took place when newly arrived captives from Africa joined with Native Americans in Natchez on the Mississippi River and killed about two hundred French settlers.

In the 1780s, when Spain ruled the territory that became the state of Louisiana, Spanish troops hunted down enslaved men who had escaped into the swamps below New Orleans. Known as maroons, these escapees had formed communities in the swamps and lived there until Spanish soldiers caught their leader, St. Maló, also known as Juan Maló. He and several of his followers were killed by hanging in New Orleans.

A slave rebellion that started in the 1790s on the nearby island of Hispaniola had a major impact on New Orleans. France had a colony called Saint-Domingue on the island. Enslaved people worked on the island's sugar plantations until Toussaint L'Ouverture led a slave rebellion that overthrew French rule, ended slavery, and re-named the colony Haiti, which became an independent country. Many of Haiti's French residents, including Homer Plessy's French grandfather, fled to Louisiana, as did many of the island's free people of color. Some escaping slaveholders brought along those they had enslaved. These newcomers helped the local economy by bringing with them a variety of sugar that grew better in Louisiana than the kind that Louisiana plantations had been growing. Some new arrivals also brought knowledge of better techniques for turning sugar cane juice into granulated sugar, which could then be sold.

However, Louisiana slaveholders feared that in addition to farming skills, enslaved newcomers might bring with them thoughts of starting an uprising. Those fears proved correct. The largest slave uprising in U.S. history took place in Louisiana in 1811. The rebellion involved about five hundred enslaved people, many of whom knew about the Haiti revolt. U.S. troops and militias made up of white plantation owners put an end to this rebellion.

Slave uprisings that took place later in Virginia, during the 1830s and 1850s, caused Louisiana's slaveholders to tighten their grip on both the enslaved and the free. A law forbade any Black people from meeting in a group without white people there to supervise. Another law made it illegal for books and newspapers to print anti-slavery messages. In 1857, the state's legislature stopped letting enslaved people buy their freedom or be freed by slaveholders. Free people of color had to carry identification papers. Journalists writing for white newspapers even suggested that people of color should be forced to leave the state. In 1859, the state legislature passed a

The Advocate, November 9, 2019, Capital City Press/Georges Media Group, Baton Rouge, LA, photo by Scott Threlkeld

In this 2019 re-enactment of the two-day march that enslaved rebels made in 1811, re-enactors walked from areas west of New Orleans along the Mississippi coastline, dressed like 1811 rebels and shouting the slogan, "On to New Orleans." Unlike the original rebels, the re-enactors reached New Orleans and celebrated the courage of the 1811 rebels with a concert in Congo Square.

law that said free people of color should choose a master and become slaves for life.

In 1857, the position of free people of color grew worse with the U.S. Supreme Court decision in the Dred Scott case. Dred Scott, an enslaved man from Virginia, filed a lawsuit to win his freedom after he was taken to a state where slavery was illegal. His original lawsuit also called for freedom for his wife, Harriet Robinson Scott, and their two children. However, the Supreme Court ruled that Dred Scott must remain enslaved. That meant his family did, too. The court also stated that no Black people, not even free people of color, could ever become U.S. citizens because they "had no rights which the white man was bound to respect."

The shocking Dred Scott decision actually led to increased rights for people of color because it outraged abolitionists,

SECRET PLANS

The largest slave uprising in U.S. history started on a sugar cane plantation on the banks of the Mississippi River, about thirty miles west of New Orleans. Led by Charles Deslondes, a small group of enslaved men from local plantations met in secret and carefully planned the rebellion. They knew about the slave revolt in Haiti. One of them, who had been captured in West Africa, still remembered tactics used by African Akan warriors. On January 8, 1811, Deslondes and others stormed the owner's mansion at one plantation, wounding the owner and killing his son. The rebels armed themselves with the plantation's guns, as well as with knives, axes, and other tools used to harvest sugar cane. For two days, they marched toward New Orleans, hoping to take over the city. About five hundred enslaved people joined along the way, burning some plantation buildings, before U.S. troops and armed plantation owners ended the uprising, brutally killing Deslondes and many rebels. Plantation owners downplayed the importance of this rebellion to help prevent a repeat. It only became better known recently with the publication of two books: *On to New Orleans!* in 1995 and *American Uprising* in 2012.

who opposed slavery. They increased their efforts to end it, which helped lead to the start of the Civil War.

In 1861, eleven southern states, including Louisiana, that wanted slavery to remain legal seceded from the rest of the nation. They formed a new country, the Confederate States of America, also called the Confederacy. Mississippi's official statement made it clear that preserving slavery was the state's reason for joining the Confederacy. The statement said, "Our position is thoroughly identified with the institution of slavery." Alexander H. Stephens, Vice President of the Confederacy, said in 1861 that the desire to continue slavery was "the immediate cause of the . . . present revolution." Louisiana's governor, Thomas Overton Moore, who supported seceding, noted that members of Congress from northern states were passing legislation that was "destroying the rights of slaveholders."

President Abraham Lincoln and northern states were determined to keep the nation together. When Confederate forces attacked U.S. Army troops at Fort Sumter in South Carolina in 1861, war began. It was the issue of slavery, most historians now agree, that so divided the nation that it led to this war that left more than 600,000 dead.

By the Civil War's end four years later, the Confederacy had been defeated and slavery abolished. A new era of rights for Black people began, thanks to three new amendments added to the U.S. Constitution. These amendments completely changed the definition of who could be a U.S. citizen and broadened the rights that all citizens could enjoy, including people of color.

New Rights Gained

The 14th Amendment, which was added to the U.S. Constitution in 1868, played a role in the 1892 courtroom meeting between the relatives of Keith Plessy and Phoebe Ferguson. This amendment overturned the unjust Dred Scott Supreme Court decision by asserting that anyone born in the U.S. was an American citizen, including people of color. It also said that a state could not make laws that would take away the rights of any citizen, and could not "deny" anyone "the equal protection of the laws." Black citizens now definitely had rights that white citizens were required to respect.

The other two new amendments also introduced major changes. The 13th Amendment, added to the U.S. Constitution in 1865, ended slavery. It fulfilled the aim of the Emancipation Proclamation issued during the war in 1863, the year Homer Plessy was born. That Proclamation had ended slavery only in the states in the Confederacy. The 13th Amendment ended slavery everywhere in the country.

In 1870, the new 15th Amendment said that no citizen could be denied the right to vote. Because the 14th Amendment had said that anyone born in the U.S. was a citizen, that meant that American-born Black men now had the right to vote. This gave people of color a feeling of hope that more change would follow. They knew that Black voters could be counted on to elect officials who would look out for their rights. No women, however, white or Black, received the right to vote until 1920, fifty years later. (See Resources at the end of the book for texts of the main sections of these three amendments.)

People of color in New Orleans had a head start in gaining rights because the Union Army defeated Confederate forces there early in the war, in April 1862. The Union Army then gave Black people in New Orleans the right to an education and set up schools for them. People of color also claimed the right to help defeat the Confederacy elsewhere by volunteering to serve in a new Black regiment of the Union Army that fought in several battles. More than forty years earlier, free men of color had volunteered in the same way to help defend New Orleans during the War of 1812. Among those earlier volunteers were two relatives of Homer Plessy: one of his grandfathers and a great uncle.

With victorious Union troops in the city, many enslaved people freed themselves in 1862, several months before the Emancipation Proclamation was issued. They sought the Union Army's protection to claim their freedom. Officials were not prepared to handle so many people eager to start new lives. The Army put some of the formerly enslaved to work on Army construction projects and sent others to plantations to work under "labor contracts" that often were unfair to the workers. Many Black people—including free people of color—were arrested if they didn't have papers proving that they had jobs or had always been free. In early 1863, the Black community sent the Army a letter protesting these arrests.

Adding to the confusion, the 1863 Emancipation Proclamation did not actually apply to New Orleans. It only freed the enslaved in those parts of the Confederacy that had *not* yet been defeated by the Union Army. Although many enslaved people freed themselves in New Orleans, slavery didn't end officially there until the next year, 1864. The Army called for an election to choose a new governor for Louisiana. In addition, delegates were to be selected for a constitutional convention that would write a new constitution for the state. Because the 15th Amendment giving Black men the right to vote had not yet been passed, the Army used the voting system from before the Civil War. That meant only white men could vote. It's no surprise that the state's newly elected gov-

Dr. Louis Charles Roudanez, who founded the newspaper L'Union *in 1862 with his brother Jean Baptiste Roudanez. The paper's name later changed to the* New Orleans Tribune. *Published initially three days a week, the* Tribune *soon became a daily newspaper.*

© The Roudanez Family Collection, Roudanez History & Legacy, www.roudanez.com

New Orleans Tribune.
A TRI—WEEKLY PAPER.

FIRST YEAR.　　　　　　NEW ORLEANS, THURSDAY, JULY 21st, 1864.　　　　　　VOL. I—No. 1.

ernor was white, as were all the delegates for the constitutional convention. Many of the delegates had supported the Confederacy. The constitution that they wrote in 1864 ended slavery, but it didn't give Black men the right to vote.

President Abraham Lincoln had earlier suggested to Louisiana's new governor that the delegates could give some Black men the right to vote: those men, Lincoln said, who were "very intelligent, and especially those who have fought gallantly" in the Union Army. Lincoln made this suggestion after meeting with Jean Baptiste Roudanez, one of the founders of *L'Union*, a new Black-owned New Orleans newspaper that had published articles about the importance of allowing Black men to vote. Roudanez had traveled to Washington in early 1864 with fellow Creole, E. Arnold Bertonneau, who had been a Union Army officer. They met with President Lincoln and gave him a petition calling for voting rights for people of color. More than a thousand New Orleans residents had signed the petition, including Michel Debergue, one of the free men of color who had served with the U.S. Army during the War of 1812. He was also the proud grandfather of a new grandson, Homer Plessy, born the previous year to his daughter Rosalie Debergue and her husband, Joseph Adolphe Plessy.

Most of the others who signed the voting rights petition were also people of color, but twenty-two white people signed as well. Not all white people in Louisiana had supported the Confederacy. About ten percent had not, and many of them supported equal rights for people of color. The petition impressed President Lincoln, but the constitutional convention's all-white delegates refused to take his suggestion about giving some Black men the vote.

In the next election, white men once again were the only voters. Candidates who had supported the Confederacy were elected to many positions. They began enforcing rules that were very much like the Black Codes that had made life diffi-

NEWSPAPERS LED THE WAY

Newspapers started by free people of color led the struggle for equal rights in New Orleans, beginning in 1862 with *L'Union*, the South's first Black newspaper, founded by two brothers: Dr. Louis Charles Roudanez, who had gone to medical school in Paris, and Jean Baptiste Roudanez, an engineer. Published three times a week, initially in French, *L'Union* demanded fair treatment and voting rights for Black men. It organized a meeting of people of color and their white supporters, which led to the voting rights petition given to President Lincoln in 1864. When that didn't win Black men the vote, Dr. Roudanez changed the newspaper to reach more people, giving it a new name, the *Tribune*, and publishing it more often, with articles in English and French. The *Tribune* was the nation's first Black daily newspaper. But by the 1870s, when many newly won rights came under attack, the *Tribune* was no longer being published. Another Black-owned newspaper soon took up the challenge, *The Crusader*, founded in 1889 by lawyer Louis A. Martinet. It led the fight against the Separate Car Act. *The Crusader*'s motto: "A Free Vote and Fair Count, Free Schools, Fair Wages, Justice and Equal Rights."

cult for people of color before the Civil War. The pro-Confederacy officials were members of that era's Democratic Party. People who supported rights for people of color were in the Republican Party, the party of President Lincoln.

Soon, people of color and their white Republican supporters came up with a way to re-open the constitutional convention in order to change the 1864 constitution so it would give Black men voting rights. They tried to hold a meeting to do this in July 1866, but a mob of armed white people attacked the building in New Orleans where voting rights supporters had gathered. Among the white attackers were former Confederate Army officers and policemen, too. They fired on more than two hundred people of color, including Union Army veterans, who had marched to the building to support Black rights. The white mob killed about forty-four people of color and injured more than a hundred. Three white supporters of Black rights also died. Union troops arrived too late to stop the slaughter. The Union Army commander, General Philip Sheridan, reported, "It was no riot. It was an absolute massacre."

This 1866 Harper's Weekly *drawing shows whites who opposed Black rights killing people of color in July 1866. The massacre took place near the building where white supporters of Black rights were trying to change the Louisiana constitution to grant Black men the right to vote.*

Courtesy Library of Congress

This massacre, and another in Tennessee, persuaded the U.S. Congress to pass new laws to protect African Americans. In addition, Congress set up military districts in the South where U.S. Army troops would try to keep the peace. These troops stayed in Louisiana and some other southern states for ten more years, a period of time known as Reconstruction. General Sheridan took charge in Louisiana. He removed Confederacy supporters from office and ordered that Black men and white men be allowed to vote in new elections in 1867.

During Reconstruction, with U.S. troops stationed in the South, people of color in New Orleans played an active role in expanding their rights. However, they faced constant opposition from armed white groups that had supported the Confederacy. Even so, there were some victories. In 1867, people of color staged protests in New Orleans that persuaded streetcar companies to stop making Black riders sit in different cars than white customers.

Another step forward came in 1868, when Louisiana passed a new constitution. This time, an equal number of Black and white delegates wrote the constitution. The 1868 constitution greatly expanded rights for people of color, including making it official that Black men could vote. It also denied voting rights to some who had supported the Confederacy, although that ban wasn't always obeyed and was overturned about ten years later.

The new 1868 constitution also permitted Black children to attend public schools together with white children. This made it more likely that children of color would receive a good education. Homer Plessy would have been old enough to start school then, but it's not known whether he attended an integrated school. At first, many white families refused to let their children attend public schools with Black students, sending their youngsters instead to private, all-white schools. By 1875, however, white enrollment in the integrated public schools had increased, often because of the low quality of the hastily organized all-white schools and their rising tuition. From then on, integrated schools seemed to be succeeding in New Orleans. It was the only southern city to have accomplished this. Not many northern cities had integrated public

Courtesy The Historic New Orleans Collection, 1979.183

These are the African American delegates who helped write the 1868 Louisiana Constitution that granted Black men the right to vote and called for integrated schools. In the center is O. J. Dunn, soon to be elected the state's Lieutenant Governor.

schools then, either. At that time, New Orleans was a leader in providing education for all.

The 1868 constitution also officially ended segregation in all businesses that served the public, as well as in all forms of transportation, including trains. But not all businesses obeyed those new requirements. Discrimination continued in many public places. People of color sometimes protested in court if they weren't served at a restaurant or allowed to sit in the better seats at a concert. A few of these cases were successful. Creole official Charles Sauvinet won his 1871 lawsuit against a restaurant that refused to serve him a drink. The court ordered the restaurant to pay Sauvinet $1,000. Not all lawsuits turned out so well. In 1872 Josephine DeCuir sued a Mississippi River steamboat company that refused to let her use one of their better rooms, which were only for white passengers. She won in two Louisiana courts. But when the steamboat company appealed these verdicts to the U.S.

An 1868 drawing from Harper's Weekly *highlighting the importance of voting, with people of color listening to a candidate's election speech.*

ELECTIONEERING AT THE SOUTH.—Sketched by W. L. Sheppard.—[See Page 467.]

Courtesy The Historic New Orleans Collection, Gift of Mr. Harold Schilke and Mr. Boyd Cruise, 1959.159.40

Supreme Court, it ruled in favor of the company and DeCuir lost her case.

Because Black men now had the right to vote, people of color were elected to office. Those serving in the state legislature helped pass laws that expanded Black rights. In 1870, the newly elected state legislature voted to allow people of different races to marry. The legislature also approved the new 14th Amendment to the U.S. Constitution, something southern states were required to do in order to rejoin the U.S.

Oscar J. Dunn won election as Louisiana's Lieutenant Governor in 1868. When he died before his term ended, another person of color replaced him: P. B. S. Pinchback, who at the time was the president of the Louisiana State Senate. In 1872, Louisiana voters elected an African American as the state's education superintendent. That same year, Pinchback became Louisiana's first Black governor after the previous governor, a white politician, was impeached due to political differences with others in Louisiana's Republican Party. Pinchback was the first African American to serve as a governor of any state.

Rising Up, Together

The 1868 constitution gave Black citizens and their white supporters a sense of hope. An interracial group of fifty Black people and fifty white people put that hope into action in 1873 by creating the Unification Movement. These idealists aimed to usher in a new era of Black and white people working together as equals. It was a high-point for the Reconstruction era in New Orleans.

Among the people of color who helped start the 1873 Unification Movement were Dr. Louis Roudanez, the *Tribune* newspaper founder; Captain Cesar (C. C.) Antoine, then the state's lieutenant governor; and Aristide Mary, a prominent Creole businessman. The group's white founders included a former Confederate Army officer, General P. G. T. Beauregard, and Mark Isaacs, a Jewish grocery store owner, who was chosen as the Unification Movement's chairman.

They wrote a statement of their beliefs: "An Appeal for the Unification of the People of Louisiana." Several local newspapers printed it in June 1873, listing the names of about eight hundred people, Black and white, who signed the statement. Among the signers was Homer Plessy's stepfather. He had raised Homer from the age of eight, after the death of Homer's father. A thousand others also signed the statement of beliefs, but newspapers didn't have room to print all those additional names.

However, this interracial effort came to an end when the Unification Movement held a huge public meeting in July 1873. White people who opposed the group's goals heckled the speakers and shouted down the idea of interracial schools. The next day, many who had signed the Unification Movement's statement stopped supporting the group. Very likely, they feared becoming the target of armed white groups that were attacking Black people and their supporters throughout the state. This marked the end of the Unification Movement's lofty attempt to bring Black people and white people together. It also marked the start of a downward spiral, as newly-won rights began to disappear.

Sliding Downward

Armed groups of white people who were determined to restore white control in Louisiana and in other southern states helped speed up the loss of rights for people of color. Groups such as the Ku Klux Klan and Louisiana's White League terrorized communities to make Black citizens afraid to vote and white citizens afraid to stand up for them. In Opelousas in St. Landry Parish, northwest of New Orleans, white mobs killed about two hundred Black people in 1868. In an 1873 assault in Colfax, in the center of the state, as many as 150 people of color were killed as they tried to prevent an armed white group from taking over the courthouse to install Democrats in office. White attackers killed many of the Black courthouse defenders after they had surrendered. In 1874, thousands of armed White League members took over the New Orleans offices of Louisiana's Republican governor, who supported Black rights. The White League wanted to replace him with a Democrat who opposed equal rights for people of color. Black and white New Orleans police officers tried to stop the takeover but were greatly outnumbered. Eleven policemen died dur-

This illustration from Frank Leslie's Illustrated Newspaper shows Black militiamen defending Louisiana's Colfax courthouse in 1873 to prevent white attackers from taking over and installing officials opposed to equal rights for people of color. When the white attackers brought a cannon to use, the Black militia surrendered, but many were still killed. As many as 150 people of color died.

Courtesy The Historic New Orleans Collection, 1995.10.4

ing this attack, which became known as the Battle of Liberty Place. When U.S. troops arrived three days after the attack began, White League fighters retreated. But later that year, White Leaguers attacked again. Some of the members were high school students, and they attacked the city's integrated schools, harassing teachers and forcing Black students to flee.

Soon, U.S. troops would no longer be on hand to defend people of color because of a deal that Rutherford B. Hayes made to become U.S. president. The presidential election of 1876 was so close that Hayes, a Republican, needed a few more votes to win in the Electoral College, the official group whose voting actually decides who becomes a U.S. president. Hayes promised Louisiana and other southern states that he would remove U.S. troops from the South if their delegates voted for him. Southerners accepted the deal, which is known as the Compromise of 1877. Once elected, Hayes followed through on his promise. In 1877, U.S. troops were pulled out of Louisiana and the two other southern states where federal troops were still on duty, South Carolina and Florida. This marked the end of Reconstruction and the start of a new era during which African Americans lost many of the rights they had won since the end of the Civil War.

With the troops gone, white Democrats who supported whites-only rule took control in Louisiana. Backroom deal-making had also occurred in Louisiana as part of the Compromise of 1877. That led to a white Democrat being declared the winner of Louisiana's close election for governor. This new governor, Francis T. Nicholls, was a former Confederate general who had the support of the White League. Two years later, another new constitution for the state officially ended the ban on Confederacy supporters voting. Many years later, in 1890, Nicholls became governor again and signed into law the legislature's Separate Car Act, the law that outraged Homer Plessy and so many others.

However, it was during Nicholls' first term as governor in 1877 that people of color lost one of their most prized new rights. A new state superintendent of education wanted to stop Black and white children from going to school together. Thirty-one prominent members of New Orleans' Black Creole community went to the statehouse to meet with Governor Nicholls to protest the plan to end integrated schools. The group included many who had been active earlier in winning rights for people of color, including Aristide Mary, Captain C. C. Antoine, Dr. Louis C. Roudanez, and Louis Martinet, a young lawyer who would soon start the new activist newspaper, *The Crusader*. The governor refused to help. He suggested they file lawsuits in court. Two Creole leaders did that. Their lawsuits claimed that separate schools for Black and white students violated the guarantee of equal protection that was part of both the U.S. Constitution and of Louisiana's 1868 constitution, too. In both cases, judges rejected the lawsuits. The white-controlled school board then did away with integrated education, which had been one of the proudest accomplishments of the Reconstruction era in New Orleans.

Putting on the Brakes

Homer Plessy was a teenager when New Orleans school integration ended. He had nearly finished his schooling by then, beginning his career as a shoemaker at age sixteen. Later, when he saw that the city's public schools for children of color weren't providing students with a good education, he joined

"IRREPARABLE INJURY"

Paul Trévigne, a Creole writer for the *L'Union* and *Tribune* newspapers, filed a lawsuit in 1877 to prevent the end of integrated schools in New Orleans. For many years, he had taught children at the Couvent School. Based on his experience as an educator, he claimed in his lawsuit that separating children by race could cause "irreparable injury to the entire colored population of the city in that it tends to degrade them as citizens by discriminating against them on account of race and color." A local judge rejected this lawsuit because Trévigne had not presented proof that segregated schools damaged Black youngsters. Captain E. Arnold Bertonneau also filed suit in 1877 when his two young sons were turned away from a New Orleans school for white students. He lost his case, too. A federal judge ruled that separating children by race didn't violate the U.S. Constitution because "both races are treated precisely alike. White children and colored children are compelled to attend different schools." Seventy-seven years later, in 1954—three years before Phoebe Ferguson and Keith Plessy were born—the U.S. Supreme Court took totally opposite stands on the arguments that Trévigne and Bertonneau had used and ruled in favor of integrated schooling.

a group that tried to make those schools better: the Justice, Protective, Educational, and Social Club. In 1887, at age twenty-four, he became this club's vice president. It issued a report calling on the school board to provide better teachers and equipment in the schools for children of color so that "we are respected, our rights protected." Sadly, the school board did not improve the schools for children of color.

Then in 1890, another setback for Black rights occurred when Louisiana's legislature passed the Separate Car Act. It required white and Black passengers to travel in separate train cars. People of color in New Orleans saw that it was time to stand up and forcefully defend their rights. They had to find a way to block the Separate Car Act so there wouldn't soon be other laws like it, taking away even more rights. Homer Plessy volunteered to help.

Courtesy Ayo Scott, photo by Amy Nathan

In 2018, New Orleans artist Ayo Scott created this image of a train engine as part of a mural about Homer Plessy's story that he painted on a wall in New Orleans' Plessy Park. In this section of the mural, the artist made all the words on the signs go backwards, reflecting how people of color must have felt when the Separate Car Act became law in 1890—that things were going backwards, with a return to segregated transportation and the possibility that even more rights might soon be lost.

WHEN A PLESSY
FIRST MET A FERGUSON

O n the first day of September 1891, a meeting at the New
Orleans office of *The Crusader* newspaper set in motion a
series of events that led to Homer Plessy coming face to face
with Phoebe Ferguson's great-great-grandfather. The eighteen
businessmen, lawyers, teachers, writers, government workers, and craftsmen who gathered there that day signed up to
be members of the Comité des Citoyens, which is French for
"Citizens' Committee." The members of this committee spent
the next five years working to overturn the Separate Car Act.

Louis Martinet, the lawyer who founded *The Crusader*
newspaper, had already suggested a way to fight the Separate
Car Act. In an editorial for his newspaper in July 1890, right
after the act became a law, he wrote: "We'll make a case, a test
case, and bring it before the Federal Courts" in order to let the
courts "test the constitutionality of the law."

A year later, on July 4, 1891, one of *The Crusader*'s regular
columnists, Rodolphe Desdunes, repeated that suggestion in
an article about the need to "defend our constitutional rights"
(mentioned in the previous chapter). In his article, Desdunes
called on the city's Republican activists to work together to
test the Separate Car Act in court. He named several well-
known local leaders who he hoped would step forward to lead

THE CRUSADER.

One Year, $1.50.	Pro Labore et Justitia.	Single Copy, 5cts.
VOL 2.	NEW ORLEANS, LA., SATURDAY, JULY 19, 1890.	No. 23.

Masthead for The Crusader *newspaper.*

Courtesy Special Collections, Howard-Tilton Memorial Library, Tulane University

the effort, including C. C. Antoine, a Union Army veteran who had been a delegate to the 1868 constitutional convention and served as the state's Lieutenant Governor for several years. Here is the challenge Desdunes made:

> We need leaders in the present emergency. . . . Appoint your committee, gentlemen, and go to work. . . . By way of encouragement we are authorized to state that many loyal hearts are waiting, ready to put their shoulders to the wheel just as soon as the car of liberty is put in motion. . . . toward the vindication of American citizenship.

One of the community's most prominent Republican activists, Aristide Mary, accepted the challenge. Years earlier, he had been part of the short-lived Unification Movement. Now in his late sixties, he urged others to join with him to form the Citizens' Committee to oppose the Separate Car Act. Educated in Paris, he was among the city's wealthiest Black Creoles. He owned a block of buildings in New Orleans that he inherited from his white father.

Most of the seventeen others who met that September day to form the Citizens' Committee were also mixed-race Creoles, with French roots. Several had been part of the Unification Movement, including Captain Antoine and Arthur Esteves, the owner of a sail-making company, an important business in a Mississippi River city. The Citizens' Committee chose Esteves as its president and Antoine as vice-president. Five Citizens' Committee members had connections to *The Crusader*, including Martinet, Desdunes, and L. J. Joubert, the newspaper's business manager.

Homer Plessy was not a member of the Citizens' Commit-

Courtesy Louisiana Division/City Archives, New Orleans Public Library

There are no photos of Louis Martinet or of most of the other members of the Citizens' Committee. Those for whom there are photos include writer Rodolphe Desdunes and the three men shown here: businessman Arthur Esteves (left), activist Laurent Auguste (center), and funeral home director, Alcee Labat.

tee, but he knew Esteves, Joubert, and Antoine from working with them in the group that was trying to improve the city's schools. Esteves was also the president of the board of the Couvent School. Others on the Committee supported the school, too.

Paul Bonseigneur, a tailor, served as the Citizens' Committee's treasurer, overseeing its fundraising efforts. This was one of the Committee's main jobs because its members chose to do what Martinet and Desdunes had suggested: Bring a test case to court. To hire a good lawyer, the Committee would need to raise money. These community leaders had concluded that arguing forcefully against the Separate Car Act in court offered a better chance of success than trying to persuade legislators who had just voted for the law to now repeal it.

The Committee hoped the court-case strategy would eventually give the U.S. Supreme Court, the nation's highest court, a chance to take a hard look at the Separate Car Act and decide whether or not it was constitutional. Committee members thought the Supreme Court's justices would surely see how blatantly the law violated the 14th Amendment's guarantee of equal protection for all. If their lawyers could persuade the Supreme Court to rule against the Separate Car Act, the Committee figured this would help put an end to any future laws that would discriminate against African Americans.

Building Wide Support

The Committee got busy right away. Four days after their first meeting, *The Crusader* newspaper published a call to action, titled "An Appeal." It explained the reasons for opposing the Separate Car Act and asked people to donate what they could. Money donations of any amount, the article explained, would help "defray judicial expenses." Contributions would also show that overturning the law had popular support, delivering the message that the power "of the poor may equal in merit the liberality of the rich."

Throughout the autumn of 1891, Committee members raised funds and also awareness within the Black community of the need to block the Separate Car Act. They walked through their neighborhoods to encourage people to sign up as supporters and make a donation. Local clubs and churches raised money to donate to the Committee. So did workers' associations, such as the Mechanics Social Club and the Bricklayers and Masons Union. Although the Citizens' Committee had no women members, women played a role in the fundraising. They held a concert to raise funds for the Committee, and women's clubs donated money as well.

Crusader articles about the Citizens' Committee reached people around the country who were interested in equal rights and regularly read this newspaper. Donations poured in from other areas of Louisiana, as well as from small towns in Mississippi, Kansas, and Illinois, and from big cities, too: San Francisco, Chicago, San Antonio, and Washington, D.C.

In just a few months, the Citizens' Committee raised $2,982—equal to raising about $84,000 today—showing many people cared deeply about getting rid of the unjust law.

Albion Tourgée, a white upstate New York lawyer, made a different kind of contribution. He offered to serve as the Citizens' Committee's legal advisor for free. A strong supporter of Black rights all his life, Tourgée left college to join the Union Army when the Civil War started. After the war, during which he was injured, he spent six years as a judge in North Carolina, deciding civil rights cases. He also helped write a new constitution for North Carolina. It gave Black citizens many of the same new rights that Louisiana's 1868 constitution did.

Albion Tourgée, who wrote above his signature: "Ignorance and neglect are the mainsprings of misrule."

Courtesy Cornell University Library

Ignorance and neglect are the mainsprings of misrule.

Albion W. Tourgée

In the 1870s, Tourgée moved to upstate New York, wrote two books, and became the author of a regular column on Black rights for a Chicago newspaper read around the country, including in New Orleans. A fan of his column who visited New Orleans wrote to Tourgée about the Separate Car Act, sparking his interest in the case. When Tourgée learned about the Citizens' Committee's "Appeal," he offered to help.

Tourgée's offer of free legal advice delighted Louis Martinet. Although Martinet was a lawyer—one of the first graduates of Straight University Law School, a new school set up in New Orleans for people of color after the Civil War—he hadn't worked as a trial lawyer in courts. In contrast, Tourgée had courtroom experience, especially with civil rights cases. Martinet hoped Tourgée's knowledge and experience would help the Committee succeed.

For the next five years, Tourgée and Martinet wrote letters back and forth between Louisiana and New York, discussing strategies. After considering various options, they chose to use the bold tactic of civil disobedience.

A PARTNERSHIP

They never met in person, but Louis Martinet and Albion Tourgée developed a warm, trusting relationship through the letters they wrote each other to plan the case against the Separate Car Act. They lifted each other's spirits when things looked bleak. Martinet wrote in 1892: "The fight we are making is an uphill one. . . . We must not lose heart."

Courtesy Chautauqua County Historical Society

A copy of a letter Louis Martinet sent to Albion Tourgée in October 1891 in which he thanked Tourgée for complimenting him but asked him not to call him a "hero." Martinet explained why: "In that way, I'll not disappoint you."

The Citizens' Committee decided to arrange for a person of color to break the law by sitting in a train car for white passengers. This would lead to an arrest. Then a lawyer hired by the Committee could explain to a judge why the Separate Car Act broke a higher law: the 14th Amendment's guarantee that all citizens should have "the equal protection of the laws."

The Volunteer

In 1892, Homer Plessy, newly married, volunteered to be arrested. His skin was so light in color that he could enter a train car for white people without others realizing he was Black. Because some of his ancestors had been white, he was said to be only about one-eighth Black. But he identified as a person of color and was willing to break the law and participate in this test case. Protesting against injustice was a family tradition. In the 1860s, his grandfather on his mother's side signed the petition that was delivered to President Lincoln, calling for the right to vote for people of color. In the 1870s, Homer Plessy's stepfather joined the short-lived Unification Movement. Homer Plessy was already standing up for equal rights himself by leading a group trying to improve schools for children of color. Now, he was ready to step up again, risking arrest to protest an unjust law.

The Citizens' Committee planned the arrest in great detail, with Louis Martinet handling most of the day-to-day organizing. He contacted train companies to find ones that would help make the arrest go smoothly. Train companies didn't like the Separate Car Act either because they had to spend money to add separate cars for Black passengers.

Martinet found people to do practice train rides to figure out how best to organize the arrest. He also found a white private detective the Committee could hire to make the actual arrest. This detective, Christopher Cain, would make sure that the volunteer was arrested for breaking the Separate Car Act, and not some other law. Then the Committee's lawyer could argue against the Separate Car Act in court.

If the Committee lost in the first court trial, they could appeal to a higher court in Louisiana and then on to the U.S. Supreme Court. If the government lost in the first trial, their lawyers would likely appeal to higher courts, too. One way or the other, the case was likely to land eventually at the U.S. Supreme Court.

On June 7, 1892, Homer Plessy went to the East Louisiana Railroad ticket office and bought a first-class ticket for a train ride from New Orleans to the nearby Louisiana town of Covington. It was important that the train would travel only inside Louisiana. Four months earlier, in February 1892, the Committee had arranged for the train-ride arrest of another volunteer, Daniel Desdunes, a young musician and the son of *Crusader* writer Rodolphe Desdunes. That effort failed because the arrest happened on a train that started in Louisiana but traveled into another state, Alabama. After Daniel Desdunes' arrest, but *before* he was brought to trial, a Louisiana court ruled in a different case that the Separate Car Act was written in such a way that it applied *only* to trips "inside Louisiana." If a train traveled into another state, then passengers didn't have to obey Louisiana's Separate Car Act. This was because making rules for travel between states was usually considered the job of the U.S. government, not each individual state.

That other court's ruling meant that Daniel Desdunes' arrest would be thrown out when it finally came to trial. A judge would say that because Desdunes' train was traveling to another state, he shouldn't have been arrested for breaking Louisiana's train law. So the Committee's lawyer would have no chance to explain to the judge about the injustice of the Separate Car Act.

That is exactly what happened when Desdunes' case did have a trial in early July. But by then the Citizens' Committee had found a new volunteer to be arrested, Homer Plessy. The Committee had also found a Louisiana-only train company that agreed to make Plessy's arrest go smoothly.

After buying a ticket on June 7, 1892, Plessy made his way to the car for white passengers and sat down. As the train started moving, the conductor came to collect tickets and, as planned, asked Homer Plessy, "Are you a colored man?"

When Homer Plessy said, "Yes," he was told to move to the car for Black travelers. He refused. The conductor had the train's engineer stop the train. It came to a halt about a block away from where Plessy had bought his ticket.

Courtesy Phoebe Ferguson

A ticket for a ride on the East Louisiana Railroad.

The conductor got off the train, walked back to the ticket office to find the Citizens' Committee's private detective, and brought him to the train car where Homer Plessy was sitting. Detective Cain told Plessy he had to move to the car for people of his race. When Plessy again refused to move, the detective pulled him off the train—at the corner of Royal Street and Press Street. The detective arrested Homer Plessy for breaking the regulations for train seating that were part of the Separate Car Act.

So far so good. The detective took Plessy to the Fifth Precinct Police Station so his arrest could be entered into the police department's records. Several Citizens' Committee members joined them at the police station, including Louis Martinet, Rodolphe Desdunes, and the Committee's treasurer, Paul Bonseigneur. They persuaded the judge to let Homer Plessy go home rather than spend the night in jail, promising that he would show up the next day in court.

On the following day, June 8, Homer Plessy went to a courtroom in downtown New Orleans with the Committee's treasurer and a local lawyer the Committee had hired to represent him. Bonseigneur paid a bail fee of $500 (about $14,000 today) so Homer Plessy would be able to stay out of jail if he agreed to come back when the court set a trial date.

The trial took place four months later, on October 13, 1892.

That's the day Homer Plessy met Phoebe Ferguson's long-ago relative, John Howard Ferguson, the judge who would decide the case.

© Liz Jurey for Preservation Resource Center

A recent photo of the stretch of tracks along which Homer Plessy took his short, history-making ride on June 7, 1892.

FOREVER LINKED
IN HISTORY

In a fifth grade classroom more than seventy years after Homer Plessy's arrest, Keith Plessy heard for the first time that that he might be related to Homer Plessy. As Keith recalled, "We were talking in class about history and civil rights cases. The teacher, Miss Waters, recognized that my name was spelled the same as Homer Plessy's. She brought a phone book into class and had the class look for Plessy in the book. She found my mother's name and a few others. Not a lot. The teacher said, 'There are only a few Plessys in the book. More likely than not you're related to Homer Plessy.'"

"Wow! I'm related to Homer Plessy," Keith remembered thinking. But he didn't find out exactly how he was related for more than thirty years. He also didn't learn many details during fifth grade about what Homer Plessy did. "All we had in that history book in class was that he refused to get out of his seat, like Rosa Parks. It was presented as some kind of random act of civil disobedience. The book mentioned the case but didn't go into the details of what it took to get him all the way to the Supreme Court, and the team of people behind him,

Lucile Hutton papers, Amistad Research Center, New Orleans, LA

This photo from 1929 shows a classroom in the elementary school that Keith Plessy would attend more than thirty years later, the Valena C. Jones Elementary School.

that it was actually a civil rights movement that was going on at that time. That the railroad worked with the Citizens' Committee to abolish the law. That was never explained in the book. I didn't learn about that until much later."

It wasn't until he was in his late thirties that Keith Plessy discovered exactly how he was related to Homer Plessy and heard about the important work of the Citizens' Committee. He learned this new information when he met Keith Weldon Medley, who was writing a book about Homer Plessy called *We as Freemen*. That same book would also help Phoebe Ferguson learn about her family's connection to the case. She too was in fifth grade when she first heard about Homer Plessy. But she didn't discover that John Howard Ferguson was her great-great-grandfather or hear about the book *We as Freemen* until she was in her forties.

Reading that book gave both Keith Plessy and Phoebe Ferguson a better understanding of what the case involving their long-ago relatives was about and what it was like in that New Orleans courtroom on the rainy Thursday morning of October 13, 1892, when their relatives met for the first time.

The Legal Argument

The Citizens' Committee decided to use a New Orleans lawyer to handle Homer Plessy's first trial. Louis Martinet had considered using a Black lawyer. But he decided it would be better to use James Campbell Walker, a white lawyer who had experience arguing cases successfully in local courts. It was Walker who represented Homer Plessy in court on October 13, 1892.

This New Orleans lawyer had been communicating by letter and telegram with the Committee's legal advisor in New York, Albion Tourgée. Together, they planned the legal arguments to use. Walker had served briefly as a private in the Confederate Army during the Civil War, something many young Louisiana men felt pressured to do in 1861, including even some young men of color. After the war, he clearly showed that he supported equal rights for Black people. He was willing to become a forceful advocate for those rights as a lawyer for Homer Plessy and the Citizens' Committee.

Walker opened his presentation in court that day by telling Judge John Howard Ferguson that the charges against Homer Plessy should be dropped because the Separate Car Act violated the 14th Amendment to the U.S. Constitution. He asked the judge for a chance to explain in more detail at another court hearing why separating people by race violated the amendment. Judge Ferguson agreed to have another court session two weeks later. So on October 28, with Homer Plessy once more in the courtroom, his lawyer tried again to persuade Judge Ferguson that the Separate Car Act was unconstitutional. Judge Ferguson took three weeks to reach a decision.

The Citizens' Committee thought they had a chance of winning. Judge Ferguson came from Massachusetts, a state that opposed slavery before the Civil War. He did not serve in the Union Army, as Albion Tourgée did, but spent the war

A drawing of Judge John Howard Ferguson.

Courtesy Phoebe Ferguson

years in Boston studying to be a lawyer. Ferguson moved to New Orleans after the Civil War, as many Northerners did, seeking job opportunities in helping the South recover from the devastation caused by the war. He found work as a lawyer in New Orleans and soon married a Louisiana woman whose father had always opposed slavery and had not supported the Confederacy. Maybe those aspects of the judge's life would make him rule against the Separate Car Act and decide in favor of treating Black people fairly.

However, after living in Louisiana for several years, John Howard Ferguson participated in an effort by white politicians to establish whites-only rule. As part of the deal that led to the removal of U.S. troops from the South in 1877, Francis T. Nicholls, a former Confederate general, claimed victory as Louisiana's governor (as described in Chapter 2). He created his own new legislature. His supporters removed an African American who had been in the legislature earlier and replaced him with Ferguson for a year. There's no evidence that Ferguson approved of the governor's white supremacist agenda. During Ferguson's year in the legislature he worked on some helpful laws, including one that would give people accused of a crime a chance to speak during their trials to defend themselves.

Governor Nicholls had another connection to Judge Ferguson and to Homer Plessy's case. In 1890, Nicholls was again the state's governor and signed the Separate Car Act into law. Shortly after that, another election took place, and Murphy Foster became the governor. He appointed Ferguson as a judge a few weeks after Homer Plessy's arrest. Before becoming governor, Foster had led the effort in the state legislature to pass the Separate Car Act. John Howard Ferguson might not have wanted to rule against the law that was liked by both the earlier Governor Nicholls and by the current governor who had just made Ferguson a judge.

But the Citizens' Committee saw a ray of hope in one of Ferguson's first rulings as a judge. This was in the July 1892 trial for the arrest of the Committee's first volunteer, Daniel Desdunes. Judge Ferguson, as expected, threw out the charges against Desdunes, noting that a state law could not set limits on travel between states.

At last, on November 18, 1892, Judge Ferguson gave his decision in Homer Plessy's case.

Homer Plessy lost.

Judge Ferguson found Homer Plessy guilty of breaking the law by sitting in a train car for white passengers.

Judge Ferguson rejected the idea that the 14th Amendment prevented states from making laws that separated people based on race. In addition, the judge claimed that it wasn't his job to rule on the "policy" in a law, but only on whether a law was carried out correctly. Judge Ferguson was wrong about that. Judges *do* have the right—and the responsibility—to see if the "policy" in a law upholds the U.S. Constitution. For many years, judges had been ruling on whether laws were constitutional or not. But Judge Ferguson took a narrow view of what a judge can do. He said that because the train company did what the Separate Car Act required—provide

"equal but separate" cars for Black and white passengers—
Homer Plessy had no right to sit in the car for white customers. "There is no pretense that he was not provided with equal
accommodation with the white passengers," said Judge Ferguson. He added that Homer Plessy "was simply deprived of the
liberty of doing as he pleased."

Judge Ferguson added that the Separate Car Act wasn't
unfair to Black people because it also placed limits on white
riders. The judge explained:

> Should a white passenger insist on going into a coach or
> compartment to which by race he does not belong, he
> would thereby render himself liable to punishment accord-
> ing to this law. There is therefore no distinction or unjust
> discrimination in this respect on account of color.

Ferguson's decision, although disappointing to the Citizens'
Committee, gave them a way to reach the U.S. Supreme
Court. First, they appealed the Ferguson decision to the Lou-
isiana Supreme Court. There the case was named *State of Lou-
isiana v. Homer Adolph Plessy*. (The "v" stands for "versus.")
The chief justice of Louisiana's Supreme Court at that time
was none other than the state's former governor and sup-
porter of the Separate Car Act, Francis T. Nicholls. He had
recently been appointed to this new position. A victory for
Homer Plessy in this court seemed unlikely. Even so, Homer
Plessy's lawyer, James Walker, did his best to explain why the
Separate Car Act violated the 14th Amendment. According to
Walker:

> The object of the 14th Amendment, setting forth the doc-
> trine of the equal protection of the law, was and is to pre-
> vent class or race legislation on the part of the several states
> of America. The Act in question stamps the colored man
> with the badge of servitude . . . and must . . . be declared
> unconstitutional.

Walker also pointed out the unfairness of letting a train conductor make the decision as to whether a person was white

In 1893, while spending the summer in Chicago to study for a second career in medicine, Louis Martinet sent an emotional letter to Albion Tourgée, writing: "I return South with a heavy heart. I have lived here [in Chicago] a new man—a freeman." He contrasted the freedom of life in Chicago with the limits he would face again when he returned to New Orleans. "You don't know what that feeling is, Judge. You may imagine it, but you have never experienced it. Knowing that you are a freeman, & yet not allowed to enjoy a freeman's liberty, rights, and privileges unless you stake your life every time you try it. To live always under the feeling of restraint is worse than living behind prison bars. My heart is constricted at the very thought of returning—it suffocates me." But he did return and kept on doing what he could to combat injustice.

or Black. That decision could lead to someone being arrested, "without constitutional due process of law."

Homer Plessy lost in this court, too.

That meant the Citizens' Committee could appeal the case to the nation's highest court, the U.S. Supreme Court in Washington, D.C. A win there would definitely put an end to the Separate Car Act and to other laws that treated African Americans unjustly, or so the Citizens' Committee hoped. But there was a risk they might not win in the U.S. Supreme Court either.

Risky Choice

Frederick Douglass, then in his seventies, warned the Citizens' Committee not to take their case to the U.S. Supreme Court. He was one of the most respected African American leaders in the country. As a young man, Douglass had escaped

Frederick Douglass.

Courtesy Library of Congress

from slavery in Maryland and become an eloquent writer and public speaker who opposed slavery and supported equal rights for African Americans. He feared that if the Citizens' Committee lost in the Supreme Court, it could set a dangerous precedent, a ruling that other courts and state governments would use to open the way for more laws limiting the rights of Black citizens. He died in 1895 and did not live to see whether his prediction proved true.

There was good reason to fear defeat at the U.S. Supreme

Court. Several of the court's recent rulings had raised questions about what the 14th Amendment meant. This amendment was a key part of the argument Homer Plessy's lawyer used. But in 1883, about ten years before Homer Plessy was arrested, the majority of justices on the U.S. Supreme Court voted to strike down the Civil Rights Law passed by Congress in 1875. This law had made it illegal for businesses to discriminate against African Americans. In its 1883 ruling, a majority of the Supreme Court's justices decided Congress didn't have the right to pass such a law. Most of the court's justices felt the 14th Amendment to the constitution *only* gave Congress the right to make laws about what a *state* could do—not about what individual *people* or *businesses* could do. It was up to each state, said the Court, to make laws about what people and businesses could do.

The Supreme Court had used similar reasoning a few years before, in 1876, in a case about the massacre that had taken place three years earlier in Colfax, Louisiana (mentioned in Chapter 2). U.S. government prosecutors tried to convict some of the Colfax attackers for breaking a U.S. law intended to prevent groups like the Ku Klux Klan from terrorizing African Americans. But in a case called *United States v. Cruikshank*, the U.S. Supreme Court let the attackers go free (including one named William Cruikshank). The Court used the same reasoning as it had in the case of the Civil Rights Law—that the 14th Amendment didn't give Congress the right to make laws about what individuals could do. Only state governments could do that. This way of thinking might make it hard for Homer Plessy's lawyer to persuade the justices that the Separate Car Act was unjust if the court felt that only state governments had the final say on what individual citizens could or couldn't do.

Even more troubling to the Citizens' Committee, in 1890 a majority of the Supreme Court justices ruled in favor of a Mississippi law similar to Louisiana's Separate Car Act. A railroad company brought this case to the Supreme Court to complain about paying a fine for not having a separate car for Black travelers on a train that passed through Mississippi on its way from Tennessee to Louisiana. The U.S. Supreme Court justices stated clearly that in reaching their decision, they didn't look into whether the law's separate seating was a "violation of personal rights." The court chose instead to do what Judge Ferguson had done—rule only on the narrow issue of whether the train company broke the law. The court said that the company had broken that Texas law by not having separate seating for Black passengers.

The Citizens' Committee saw a glimmer of hope. There might still be a chance to persuade the court to consider the wider issue that it had neglected to look at during the Mississippi train law case: whether separate cars for Black customers were indeed a "violation of personal rights." In addition, three new justices from northern states had joined the Supreme Court after the Mississippi case. Maybe Homer Plessy's lawyers could persuade the new justices of the unfairness of the Separate Car Act and those justices would influence the others.

Both Louis Martinet and Albion Tourgée hoped that news reports about their case might help change public opinion—and also change the opinions of the court's justices. As Tourgée noted in a letter to Martinet in 1893:

> . . . if we can get the ear of the Country, and argue the matter fully before the people first, we may incline the wavering to fall on our side when the matter comes up.

A year earlier, Martinet wrote to Tourgée about another benefit of keeping on with the case:

> The people of the North must be educated to conditions in the South . . . We must expose continually to the people of the North the hideous sores of the South & the ever-recurring outrages to which we are subjected.

Win or lose, Martinet, Tourgée, Homer Plessy, and the Citizens' Committee decided to keep going all the way to the top. It was at the U.S. Supreme Court that the family names of Keith Plessy and Phoebe Ferguson became linked forever. There, the case became known as: *Plessy v. Ferguson*.

"JOIN HANDS AND HEARTS"

In a letter to Louis Martinet in 1893, Albion Tourgée wrote that it was important that they work together to defeat the Separate Car Act: "The colored man and those white men who believe in liberty and justice—who do not think Christ's teachings a sham—must join hands and hearts and win with brain and patience and wisdom and courage . . . for the special good of your people and the general advancement of all that American liberty professes . . . in some sense, the initiative, must come from your people. . . . Those of us who already believe must join with you and echo this appeal so that it shall be heard by all the world. Without both united, there is no hope of success."

Courtesy Ayo Scott, photo by Amy Nathan

The idea of "justice" is often portrayed as a woman wearing a blindfold and holding a set of scales, weighing the evidence on either side of a dispute. Such an image suggests that justice should be blind, not influenced by outside pressures, but only by considering what is just and fair. In 2018, New Orleans artist Ayo Scott painted this image of justice as part of his mural in the city's Plessy Park. By showing a young Black man wearing a blindfold and holding scales, the artist is wondering, as he explains on his website, "what might liberty and justice look like through the eyes of another person."

COURTROOM SHOWDOWN

Homer Plessy wasn't at the U.S. Supreme Court on April 13, 1896, when the court considered the *Plessy v. Ferguson* case. Neither was Judge John Howard Ferguson. Their lawyers were there, however, presenting each side's point of view. An appearance before the Supreme Court called for a lawyer with a national reputation, and so Albion Tourgée served as Homer Plessy's main lawyer. He made the same basic point in his presentation that had been used in both of the earlier trials—that the Separate Car Act violated the 14th Amendment's guarantee that all citizens, regardless of race, should be treated equally under the law. This amendment, Tourgée said, had changed the definition of who could be a citizen:

> The old citizenship of the United States was determined by race ... Under the pre-existing law no man having a drop of colored blood in his veins, could become a citizen of the United States. It was in all literalness a "white man's government." ... In the new citizenship color is expressly ignored and the sole condition of citizenship, is birth in the United States.

Tourgée noted also that the 13th Amendment had abolished slavery, but separating Black people from white people in public continued the idea of white superiority, which had been a central feature of slavery. So he felt that the Separate Car Act violated the 13th Amendment, too. In addition, he shared with the court something that New Orleans lawyer James Walker had discovered: Louisiana had no law defining "white" and "colored." Tourgée asked, "How shall a man who may have one-eighth or one-sixteenth colored blood know to which race he belongs? The law does not tell him." The Separate Car Act left that decision up to the whim of a train conductor, with no legal way for a person to challenge the decision. This, Tourgée explained, violated the 14th Amendment's guarantee that a state should not "deprive any person of life, liberty, or property, without due process of law."

In Homer Plessy's first trial, Judge John Howard Ferguson had suggested that the Separate Car Act wasn't unfair to Black people because white people could be arrested, too, if they entered the car for Black passengers. Tourgée tried to poke holes in that argument during his remarks at the Supreme Court. He said that the Separate Car Act only *pretended* to treat Black and white people equally. Its real purpose, Tourgée explained, was to maintain white superiority for people who object to sitting near a Black person. He explained:

> The Statute itself is a skillful attempt to confuse and conceal its real purpose. It assumes impartiality. . . . Its real object is to keep negroes out of one car for the gratification of the whites—not to keep whites out of another car for the comfort and satisfaction of the colored passenger.

Tourgée used a dramatic image to support his arguments, saying: "Justice is pictured blind and her daughter, the Law, ought at least to be color-blind."

His presentation did not win over a majority of the justices. Homer Plessy lost again.

On May 18, 1896, seven of the eight U.S. Supreme Court justices who voted on this case decided in favor of the rulings the Louisiana courts had made earlier—that Homer Plessy was guilty of breaking the law by sitting in a train car for white passengers.

In the statement that the justices wrote giving their opinion on the case, the phrase "equal but separate" appears at the beginning, in a section explaining what the Separate Car Act requires a train company to do. This opinion statement then describes examples of other states and cities that allow "equal but separate accommodations" for Black people and white people. The opinion concludes that separating people by race does not violate the 14th Amendment.

The seven justices reached this conclusion by using their own interpretation of the 14th Amendment. They guessed at what those who wrote the amendment probably meant but didn't actually state in the amendment. According to those seven justices, the 14th Amendment applied only to *legal* matters, such as making contracts for businesses. They felt that the amendment had nothing to do with everyday social life. To them, the purpose of the amendment:

> was undoubtedly to enforce the absolute equality of the two races before the law, but, in the nature of things, it could not have been intended to ... enforce social ... commingling of the two races upon terms unsatisfactory to either.

Those seven white male justices seemed unable—or unwilling—to see the situation from the point of view of a person of color. They could not understand why African Americans might feel discriminated against if they were found unfit to sit next to white people. The justices' statement said that if Black people feel that:

> the enforced separation of the two races stamps the colored race with a badge of inferiority ... it is not by reason of anything found in the [Separate Car] Act, but solely because the colored race chooses to put that construction upon it.

Solo Dissenter

One Supreme Court justice disagreed with the others: Justice John Marshall Harlan, one of two Southerners among the justices who heard this case. Born and raised in Kentucky,

Studio of Mathew Brady, Collection of the Supreme Court of the United States

*Justice John
Marshall Harlan*

Justice Harlan and his family had been slaveholders. When the Civil War began, he wanted slavery to continue. Even so, he joined the Union Army because he didn't want to see the nation divided. After the war, he at first was not pleased with the new amendments to the U.S. Constitution that ended slavery and granted equal rights to African Americans. But gradually, he came to see that those amendments were just.

After he was appointed to the Supreme Court in 1877, Justice Harlan often spoke out in favor of those civil rights amendments. In 1883, he was the only Supreme Court justice to disagree with the others when they overturned the Civil Rights Law that Congress had passed. The other justices felt the 14th Amendment only gave Congress the right to make laws about what states could do, not about what individual people or businesses could do (as noted in Chapter 4). In contrast, Harlan wrote that the 14th Amendment allowed Congress to pass laws "to protect the citizen . . . against discrimination on account of his race." He was also one of two justices who disagreed with the others in 1890 when the Supreme Court gave its approval to Mississippi's separate train car law.

Now, with the *Plessy v. Ferguson* case, this white Southerner realized how unjust Louisiana's Separate Car Act was. He wrote an eloquent "dissent" to protest the decision the other seven justices had reached. His essay began by commenting on the three new amendments added to the U.S. Constitution after the Civil War, noting those amendments "were welcomed by the friends of liberty throughout the world. They removed the race line from our governmental systems." He went on to explain:

In view of the Constitution, in the eye of the law, there is in this country no superior, dominant, ruling class of citizens. There is no caste here. Our Constitution is color-blind, and neither knows nor tolerates classes among citizens. In respect of civil rights, all citizens are equal before the law.

Justice Harlan gave a warning about what would happen if racial issues continued to divide the nation's citizens:

The destinies of the two races in this country are indissolubly linked together, and the interests of both require that the common government of all shall not permit the seeds of race hate to be planted . . . We boast of the freedom enjoyed by our people above all other peoples. But it is difficult to reconcile that boast with a state of the law which . . . puts the brand of servitude and degradation upon a large class of our fellow citizens. . . . The thin disguise of "equal" accommodations for passengers in railroad coaches will not mislead anyone, nor atone for the wrong this day done.

Harlan feared that laws like the Separate Car Act will make "peace impossible" in relations between Black and white citizens. He warned, as Frederick Douglass had years earlier in advising the Citizens' Committee, that if the Supreme Court justices approved of the Separate Car Act, their decision would lead to other laws separating people by race. This, Harlan noted, would "interfere with the full enjoyment of the blessings of freedom . . . and to place in a condition of legal inferiority a large body of American citizens."

In another section in his dissent, he referred to a recent U.S. law, the 1882 Chinese Exclusion Act. He noted that Louisiana's Separate Car Act would let people from China sit in a white train car even though the Chinese Exclusion Act said that Chinese people could never become U.S. citizens. Yet Louisiana's Separate Car Act prevented actual U.S. citizens— Black people born in the U.S.—from sitting in the white car. To Harlan, this showed how absurd the Separate Car Act was. He did not, however, comment on the racism of the Chinese Exclusion Act, which was not overturned for more than sixty years.

Justice Harlan also made a dramatic prediction about the *Plessy v. Ferguson* decision:

> In my opinion, the judgment this day rendered will, in time, prove to be quite as pernicious as the decision made by this tribunal in the *Dred Scott Case.*

COLOR-BLIND JUSTICE

"Justice is pictured blind," said Albion Tourgée in his *Plessy v. Ferguson* comments. Justice John Marshall Harlan picked up on that image in his dissent, in which he wrote, "Our Constitution is color-blind." The idea that justice is a woman goes back to ancient times when the Greeks had a goddess of justice. For hundreds of years, statues representing justice showed a woman with eyes open. In the 1550s, statues began to show her with a blindfold, to suggest that justice is impartial. Often she carries scales, to weigh the evidence in a case. During the *Plessy* case, the Supreme Court met in a room at the Capitol Building. In 1935, the Supreme Court moved to its own new building. At the main entrance is a small statue of a blindfolded woman with a set of scales. Blindfolded women also appear on lightposts in front of the building.

Courtesy Fred Schilling, Collection of the Supreme Court of the United States

This small statue of a blind-folded Lady Justice (above left) is held in the hands of a woman (above right) who sits at the top of the front staircase of the current U.S. Supreme Court building (below), which opened in 1935. Blindfolded women also appear on light posts in front of the court building.

Courtesy Franz Jantzen, Collection of the Supreme Court of the United States

Justice Harlan's prediction turned out to be correct.

Unfortunately for Homer Plessy, it was the other seven justices who decided his fate. There is no way to appeal a U.S. Supreme Court decision. Homer Plessy had to return to court in New Orleans and pay a $25 fine or spend twenty days in jail. He paid the fine.

"Still Believe That We Were Right"

Some who had led the fight against the Separate Car Act retired from the front lines of activism after the Supreme Court defeat. Albion Tourgée, discouraged that his arguments failed to persuade more of the justices, wrote in a letter to his wife in 1896, "I have nothing to say that the world cares to hear." He left the country the next year to take a foreign service job as a U.S. Consul in France. He died there in 1905. Louis Martinet closed his *Crusader* newspaper after the Supreme Court defeat, partly for financial reasons, but also because protest journalism seemed risky in an era when armed white militias were continuing to attack people of color. He went back to work as a lawyer and a doctor until his death on June 7, 1917, exactly twenty-five years after Homer Plessy's arrest.

Homer Plessy stopped making shoes because big factories had taken over that task. He worked as a laborer and then as a clerk for an insurance company. He also volunteered with community organizations. He died in New Orleans in 1925, having outlived Judge John Howard Ferguson by a decade. The judge had died at age seventy-seven, in 1915.

The Citizens' Committee was aware of the warning that Frederick Douglass had given them. He had feared what might happen if they lost at the Supreme Court, that a defeat there would lead to many more laws limiting the rights of people of color. But the Citizens' Committee still felt proud of what they had tried to do. As Rodolphe Desdunes noted, "We think it is more noble and dignified to fight, no matter what, than to show a passive attitude of resignation."

Before the Committee disbanded, they issued a report describing their efforts to fight the Separate Car Act. The report concluded:

In the name of the people, the Citizens' Committee battled for equal rights. . . . we, as freemen, still believe that we were right and our cause is sacred.

The ideas that the Citizens' Committee, Louis Martinet, Rodolphe Desdunes, Albion Tourgée, and Homer Plessy believed in so strongly would ultimately win at the U.S. Supreme Court, but not for more than fifty years—not until 1954, three years before the birth of Keith Plessy and Phoebe Ferguson.

Courtesy the Charles L. Franck Studio Collection at The Historic
New Orleans Collection, 1979.325.6222

*This 1951 photo of a New Orleans streetcar shows wooden signs called
"race screens." African Americans were allowed to sit only in rows that were
behind the race screen, which said "For Colored Patrons Only." The rest of
the seats were for white passengers. People of color in New Orleans thought
that streetcar segregation had come to an end in 1867. But in 1902, streetcar
segregation returned when a new law required separate streetcars for Black
and white passengers. A 1928 law extended segregation to buses. "Race screens"
were introduced so that everyone could ride in the same streetcars and buses, as
long as white passengers sat in the front and Black passengers in the back. Race
screens were used until 1958.*

THE RISE AND FALL OF "SEPARATE-BUT-EQUAL"

"That a part of my family helped start Jim Crow is kind of a load to carry," Phoebe Ferguson admitted. "I wish I could change that." After the Supreme Court's *Plessy v. Ferguson* decision, unjust laws spread across the South like wildfire, as Frederick Douglass had feared. "The suffering that resulted from that decision was a national disaster," said Keith Plessy.

The new laws came to be known as Jim Crow laws, named for an insulting term for African Americans that had been popularized by white minstrel show performers in the mid-nineteenth century. White people who wanted to roll back equal rights for African Americans now had a catchy phrase to use: "separate-but-equal." These words, lifted from the *Plessy v. Ferguson* decision and slightly re-arranged, gave white officials the Supreme Court's stamp of approval to pass laws that separated people by skin color. Those officials would claim that separate facilities for Black people were equal to those provided for white people. In most cases, that was not true. Even so, state governments enforced those Jim Crow laws, with arrests likely if not obeyed. In addition, white-owned businesses often set up their own Jim Crow rules that placed additional restrictions on African Americans. Disobeying a business's rules could lead to arrests, too (as described in the next chapter).

Jim Crow laws and rules reached into parts of the North, too. They took people of color on a painful voyage back in time, forcing them to face many of the same unjust situations that existed before the Civil War.

Phoebe was in her forties when she discovered that Judge Ferguson was her great-great-grandfather. By that time, she knew enough about civil rights history to realize that the *Plessy v. Ferguson* Supreme Court decision had led to the rules that prevented her as a child from sitting in a movie theater or riding a carousel with her African American babysitter. She was shocked to learn that her own great-great-grandfather played a part in the spread of Jim Crow. "Nobody had talked about it at home," she noted. "My mother was a big liberal and tried to help Black women get the vote in New Orleans and was on the right side of trying to integrate the schools there." Phoebe is sure that if her mother had known that Judge Ferguson was a relative, she would have said something about it. "My father's family was very conservative. My father was an only child. He died young. I don't think my dad knew, or if he did, he kept it quiet. It wasn't mentioned in my father's obituary in the newspaper when he died, that he was related to the judge."

The rules and laws that puzzled Phoebe and Keith as youngsters were just a small part of Jim Crow's reach. Separate-but-UN-equal affected nearly all aspects of life in New Orleans, as the following paragraphs show.

- *Jim Crow transportation:* In addition to separate train cars for Black and white riders, a 1902 law required separate streetcars. Soon, the use of moveable wooden signs called "race screens" allowed everyone to sit in the same streetcar or bus, with white people sitting in front and Black people sitting behind the race screen, with its message "For Colored Patrons Only." White people, including children, could move the sign whenever they wanted, sometimes moving it so far back that there was hardly any room for Black passengers. In addition, laws also required separate bus and train station waiting rooms and separate rest rooms.
- *Jim Crow Schools:* The separate public schools for children of color had lower-quality equipment than the schools for

This 1951 New Orleans photo shows that during the Jim Crow era there were even separate entrances at doctors' offices for white people and people of color.

Courtesy the Charles L. Franck Studio Collection at The Historic New Orleans Collection, 1979.325.4143

white children. Black students often had to use old textbooks that had been discarded by the schools for white students. In 1920, Louisiana was spending about seven times more on education for white children than for children of color, with $25.37 per pupil spent on white students compared to $3.49 for Black students. Until 1913, schools for children of color in Louisiana went only up to fifth grade. New Orleans' first public high school for Black students didn't open until 1917, making it hard for young African Americans to receive the kind of education that would prepare them for high-level jobs.

In addition, there wasn't a public elementary school for children of color in a major Black neighborhood, the 7th Ward, until a community group started one. This neighborhood group, with help from Beecher Memorial Congregational United Church of Christ, rented a building in 1911 to use as an elementary school for 7th Ward youngsters.

About fifty years later, Keith Plessy attended this school. By then it was in a big, new building that community leaders persuaded the city to build in 1929. (More on this in Chapter 10.)

Religious schools also helped fill in some of the educational shortcomings of the public schools. So did universities that offered high school level instruction for people of color, as well as more advanced courses. Two of these universities began during Reconstruction: Straight University, founded in 1869 by the American Missionary Association; and Leland University, founded in 1871 by the American Baptist Home Missionary Society.

- *Jim Crow in other public spaces:* There were separate water fountains for white people and Black people, separate ticket windows at the circus, separate bibles for witnesses to put their hands on when they promised to tell the truth in court, and separate treatment rooms in hospitals. Some stores had a particularly insulting Jim Crow rule: not letting African Americans try on clothes before purchasing them. There were also whites-only hotels, restaurants,

Separate Jim Crow waiting rooms occurred throughout the South, including at this North Carolina bus station.

museums, libraries, sports teams, swimming pools, parks, and beaches.

- *Jim Crow Mardi Gras:* Mardi Gras "krewes" were whites-only for many years. Krewes are the social clubs that hold parties and parades in New Orleans during Mardi Gras, the lively festival that occurs each year about six and a half weeks before Easter. In 1895, people of color created their own social club, the Illinois Club, which began holding fancy-dress balls during Mardi Gras. In 1901, people of color began marching informally in Mardi Gras parades. In 1909, the Zulu Social Aid and Pleasure Club was the first African American social club to march in a Mardi Gras parade. Most krewes remained whites-only. It wasn't until 1992 that a New Orleans law ended segregation in Mardi Gras krewes.
- *Jim Crow's impact on marriage:* Interracial marriage became illegal again in 1894. That year, Louisiana's legislature passed a new law that overturned the Reconstruction-era law of 1870 which had allowed interracial marriage. The 1894 marriage ban continued until 1967 when the U.S. Supreme Court made interracial marriage legal throughout the U.S., with its ruling in the case *Loving v. Virginia.*

Guaranteeing Jim Crow a Future

In 1898, Louisiana officials created another new constitution for the state, repealing many of the equal rights gains of the Reconstruction-era constitution of 1868. The new 1898 constitution introduced restrictions that helped guarantee that Jim Crow's grip on public life would continue for many years. One new restriction made it almost impossible for African Americans to register and vote. Preventing Black men from voting made it likely that politicians who opposed rights for Black people would be the ones elected to office. White officials openly admitted their reason for trying to keep Black men from voting. Louisiana's governor (the one who made John Howard Ferguson a judge) said the new voting regulations in the state's 1898 constitution meant that: "White supremacy for which we have so long struggled . . . is now crystallized into the [Louisiana] constitution."

THE "ORIGINAL JIM CROW"

1830s white minstrel-show performers turned the name "Jim Crow" into an insulting term for Americans of African descent. White entertainers blackened their faces with burnt cork and sang a song called "Jump Jim Crow" that depicted Black people as buffoons who trick enslavers. T. D. Rice, the white song-and-dance man who made the song a hit, learned to dance as a boy in the early 1800s by watching Black farm workers hold dance contests at a New York City market. Before 1827, when slavery ended in New York, those farm workers would have been enslaved. African folklore often features a trickster—sometimes a crow—who outsmarts the powerful. Rice may have picked up ideas for his "Jump Jim Crow" routines from watching Black dancers act out the story of a trickster. Some stories say he heard an old African American man sing a song about a character named Jim Crow. However Rice came up with the tune, he wrote many verses for it. Advertising himself as the "Original Jim Crow," he portrayed a crude character that distorted African culture, and whose name became linked to the unjust laws that oppressed that culture's descendants.

In order to vote, according to the new 1898 constitution, men had to be able to read well enough to complete a tricky reading test. They also had to own enough property to pay property taxes. For Black men who had been enslaved before the Civil War and had been prevented from learning to read and earning enough money to own property, those new requirements would keep many of them from voting. However, the regulations didn't prevent poor, uneducated white men from voting because of a special clause in the constitution: the "grandfather clause." It said that men who had been allowed to vote *before 1867*—and their sons and *grandsons*—could vote, even if they couldn't read well or didn't own property. Because no Black men could vote in Louisiana before 1867, this clause applied only to white men. The new voting plan achieved the governor's goal. Before it went into effect, nearly half of Louisiana voters were Black. By 1910, less than one percent were Black.

The 1898 constitution also reinforced the New Orleans school board's decision in the late 1870s to stop letting Black and white students go to school together. The 1898 constitution now *required* that there be separate schools for Black and white young people. Limiting the quality of the schools for children of color and having those schools cover only the early grades (as described earlier) also played a role in suppressing the Black vote. Editorial writers for the white-owned New Orleans *Daily Picayune* newspaper explained why in a 1908 issue of the paper:

> ... ability to read and write is one of the requirements of admission to suffrage [voting] in this State, and inability to comply with it shuts out the great body of the negro vote and a considerable number of whites. Just as soon as all the negroes in the State shall be able to read and write they will become qualified to vote, and it is not to be doubted that they will demand their rights ... with the Fourteenth Amendment of the Federal Constitution to back them up. Then there will be negro majorities in a great number of the parishes and wards of the State with no legal means of neutralizing or defeating that most dangerous situation.

New Jury Rules

The 1898 Jim Crow constitution introduced another new problem for people of color by changing Louisiana's jury rules. In the U.S., if someone is accused of a felony—a serious crime—there is a trial with a jury of twelve people who decide if the person is guilty. In nearly every other U.S. state, all twelve jury members have to agree for someone to be found guilty of a felony. That was true in Louisiana, too, before 1898. But the new 1898 constitution said only *nine* jury members had to agree, making it easier to convict someone.

Officials changed the jury rule for the same reason they changed the voting rules—to protect white control. Because the 14th Amendment to the U.S. Constitution had declared that Black people were citizens, that meant they could serve on juries. In addition, a U.S. Supreme Court ruling in 1880, in a case from West Virginia, held that a law *preventing* a Black juror from serving on a jury violated the "equal protection of the laws" section of the 14th Amendment. But there was nothing in the 14th Amendment saying that juries must include Black jurors nor how many there had to be. With the new nine-vote jury rule, Louisiana officials hoped that even if there were as many as three Black jurors for a court case, those jurors could not stop nine white jurors who were determined to convict someone. The votes of a few Black jurors would thus not matter in deciding a person's guilt or innocence.

When the nine-vote jury rule first went into effect, it had devastating consequences for people of color. Police at that time often arrested Black people for minor offenses. Because the nine-vote jury rule made convictions easier, increasing numbers of African American men became prisoners and found themselves in a situation very much like slavery. After the Civil War, Louisiana had set up a "convict leasing" deal with a wealthy landowner. This happened in other southern states as well. Louisiana prisoners had to work without pay on that landowner's plantation, which was named Angola (the African homeland of some enslaved people). This new form of unpaid forced labor was legal because of a surprising clause in the 13th Amendment to the U.S. Constitution, the same amendment that ended slavery. The clause says slavery is illegal "except as a punishment for crime."

Convict leasing ended in 1901 in Louisiana, shortly after the death of that landowner. But for many years, prisoners continued working under the same harsh conditions, harvesting sugar cane at the plantation. By then, it had become the state's maximum security prison, Angola Penitentiary. Even today inmates there still work under harsh conditions in the fields, harvesting sugar cane and other crops.

Conditions weren't much better after the Civil War for Black farm workers who weren't prisoners. Often, their low wages weren't paid in cash, but in coupons to use at a plantation's store. Sugar plantation workers tried to form a union and went on strike in 1887 to demand more pay. White militias put an end to that. They attacked the strikers in Thibodaux, southwest of New Orleans, killing sixty African Americans in what is known as the Thibodaux Massacre. It would be fifty years before southern Black farm workers tried to form a union again.

By 2018—more than a hundred years after the 1898 Louisiana constitution established the split-decision jury rule—Louisiana's voters decided that this rule had to go. It had already been modified so that ten jurors had to agree for a conviction. That still seemed unjust. A majority of Louisiana voters approved an amendment to the state constitution in 2018 that required a unanimous decision by all twelve jurors for a felony conviction. At that time, all other states, except Oregon, had that policy. In 2020, the U.S. Supreme Court ruled that from then on all states, including Oregon, must require unanimous jury votes for felony convictions.

Causing Damage to Neighborhoods

Jim Crow attitudes affected the housing market, too. A 1912 Louisiana law aimed to keep neighborhoods segregated. Under this law, officials could refuse to give a building permit to anyone, white or Black, who wanted to build a house in a neighborhood whose residents were of a different race from the would-be homeowner. About ten years later, another Louisiana law made it illegal in cities and large towns to rent an apartment to a person of one race if the building had tenants of a different race. In 1927, the U.S. Supreme Court overturned a Louisiana law requiring segregated neighborhoods, saying that the law violated the 14th Amendment. But Black homeowners' problems continued because of a new U.S. government agency that started in 1933: the Home Owners' Loan Corporation (HOLC).

HOLC was supposed to help homeowners who had major financial problems caused by the Great Depression, the nationwide economic downturn that began in 1929. Instead, HOLC's actions reflected the Jim Crow era's negative attitude toward African American communities. The agency prepared maps of neighborhoods in 239 cities, including New Orleans. HOLC used different colors on its maps to indicate which neighborhoods were worth investing in, such as with loans to help homeowners cover mortgage payments or make home repairs. Green and blue areas on the map showed the best neighborhoods for investment. Yellow highlighted neighborhoods that were "declining." Red areas on the maps marked neighborhoods that HOLC called "hazardous," where it could be risky for banks to invest.

"Redlined" neighborhoods generally were home to Black, poor, and working-class families. For decades, people in redlined areas had a hard time getting loans from banks and government agencies to buy a house or fix it as needed. Redlining put home-ownership out of reach for many African Americans. They also had trouble buying homes in the "better" green and blue areas, which tended to be whites-only. In addition, insurance companies and banks often made buying insurance and obtaining loans more expensive for people of color than for white people.

In 1968, the U.S. Congress outlawed redlining and racial discrimination in housing with the Fair Housing Act. But by then much damage had already been done. That damage

Courtesy Library of Congress

This Mississippi movie theater had the same Jim Crow rule as the New Orleans theater that Phoebe Ferguson and her babysitter visited in the early 1960s. The rule required people of color to sit upstairs, while white customers could sit downstairs (as described in Chapter 1).

continues to have an impact today. Many formerly redlined neighborhoods still struggle. Owning a home is one of the main ways that families can accumulate wealth, but redlining made that impossible for many people of color. Experts feel that the redlining policies of the past can help explain today's "wealth gap" between Black and white families. The net worth of white families is now nearly ten times greater than that of Black families. In 2016 in New Orleans, where about sixty percent of the population is African American, Black households "earned 47 percent less than white households," according to the New Orleans Prosperity Index.

Harming Health, Too

Recent research has shown that Jim Crow's legacy has harmed the health of people of color. Redlined neighborhoods—often areas where families of color live—tend to be areas that are close to sources of air pollution, such as the petrochemical manufacturers in the New Orleans area. Long term exposure to high levels of air pollution can make people more likely to have heart disease, asthma, and other serious health conditions. African Americans in the U.S. are also more likely than white Americans to die from heart disease or cancer, and they are more likely to develop diabetes.

In addition, researchers have found that the stress of a lifetime of coping with racist attitudes that linger from the Jim Crow era can damage the health of people of color. Always being on guard against possible mistreatment because of skin color can wear a person down. The stress can lower an individual's ability to fight off disease and may account for some of the health differences between Black and white communities. This kind of stress is sometimes called "weathering." It was described in a 2006 article by Dr. Arline Geronimus, a researcher at the University of Michigan. Also troubling, a 2003 study by the National Academy of Sciences found that people of color often receive poorer-quality medical care than white people. This can occur partly because of attitudes left over from the Jim Crow era that health care professionals may not even realize that they have. That study has prompted health care providers to become more aware of the unconscious biases that their employees may have absorbed, simply from living in a country once ruled by Jim Crow. The *Plessy v. Ferguson* decision's negative impact on people of color has reached far and wide and continues to influence attitudes and affect people's lives today.

Protests Continued

Despite all the obstacles and restrictions that Jim Crow imposed, people of color continued to protest, although doing so could lead to arrest, beatings, or death. This was especially true in the early years after the *Plessy v. Ferguson* decision, when

THE GRANDFATHER CLAUSE

The phrase "grandfather clause" first appeared in the 1890s as a way to describe voting rules in Louisiana and other southern states. Those rules said the states' voting requirements didn't apply to men whose grandfathers had been able to vote before 1867. This was a sneaky way of saying only white men didn't have to obey the rules, because Black men weren't allowed to vote in the South before 1867. The NAACP encouraged people in Oklahoma to challenge their state's grandfather clause. This led to the U.S. Supreme Court ruling in 1915 that the grandfather clause was unconstitutional for violating the 15th Amendment (which gave Black men the right to vote). Oklahoma officials tried to get around that decision, but the Supreme Court stopped them. However, there were still other ways to keep Black people from voting: charging a poll tax or giving confusing reading tests to people of color, while letting white people skip the test or saying they passed even if they didn't. In 2014, Harvard students tried out a 1964 Louisiana Voter Literacy Test. They failed to answer correctly its thirty tricky questions in the ten minutes allowed by the test's rules. In 1964, the new 24th amendment to the U.S. Constitution outlawed poll taxes. In 1965, the U.S. Congress passed the Voting Rights Act, which did away with grandfather clauses, literacy tests, poll taxes, and other voting obstacles. In recent years, however, new voting obstacles have appeared and activists are looking for ways to combat them.

armed white groups continued to terrorize Black communities. In 1909, a new organization was founded whose purpose was to support those who stand up for justice: the NAACP (National Association for the Advancement of Colored People). From the start, it has used the same strategy that Louis Martinet and the Citizens' Committee used in fighting the Separate Car Act: battle against injustice in court. Soon, the NAACP began winning court cases, including in Louisiana.

But it wasn't until 1954, three years before Keith Plessy and Phoebe Ferguson's birth, that the NAACP scored a victory that was big enough and important enough to mark the beginning of the end of the Jim Crow era. However, as Keith and Phoebe noticed as children, even after that major victory, Jim Crow attitudes had a way of sticking around.

Courtesy Ayo Scott, photo by Amy Nathan

This panel from Ayo Scott's mural at Plessy Park in New Orleans highlights an important civil rights milestone that occurred three years before the birth of Keith Plessy and Phoebe Ferguson.

HOMER PLESSY—
VINDICATED

N AACP lawyer A. P. Tureaud led the legal battle in mid-20th century New Orleans to undo the damage caused by the *Plessy v. Ferguson* Supreme Court decision. He also played a role in creating the elementary school that Keith Plessy attended as a child.

Named Alexander Pierre, but known as A. P., he grew up in New Orleans but went to high school in Washington, D.C. When he was a teenager, there was not yet a public high school for people of color in New Orleans. After earning a law degree at Washington's Howard University, he returned to New Orleans in 1925, the year Homer Plessy died.

There were few African American lawyers in New Orleans then. Although Tureaud and other Black lawyers could argue cases in court, the local lawyers' associations would not let them become members. That didn't stop Tureaud. He offered his services to the Black community. Before long, he joined the NAACP and kept filing lawsuits that chipped away at different aspects of Jim Crow. In addition, he encouraged Black people to register and vote, despite the obstacles. In 1942, he helped Black teachers gain the right to earn the same pay as white teachers. In 1950, he helped Black students win the

New Orleans civil rights lawyer, A. P. Tureaud, Sr.

Courtesy A. P. Tureaud, Jr.

right to attend law school at Louisiana State University (LSU). The first Black LSU law school graduate, Ernest (Dutch) Morial, became New Orleans' first Black mayor in 1978. He attended the same elementary school that Keith Plessy would attend later.

In 1953, Tureaud won a personal lawsuit that let his son, A. P. Tureaud, Jr., become the first Black student to register as an undergraduate at LSU. However, LSU appealed that decision and another court ruled against admitting the younger Tureaud. In the short time that he was at the university, he was harassed and shunned by white students. He then enrolled in Xavier University, a historically Black university in New Orleans, and had a distinguished career as an educator. It wasn't until 1964 that a group of African Americans successfully managed to enroll at LSU as undergraduates.

Despite that personal setback in 1953, the elder Tureaud continued to file new civil rights court cases. A lawsuit he had started in 1952 against the New Orleans school board was making its way through the courts. This lawsuit aimed to put an end to separate schools for Black and white youngsters in the city.

But before a court could reach a decision on this New Orleans school board case, the NAACP's national legal team brought a major complaint about school segregation to the U.S. Supreme Court. This case became known as *Brown v. Board of Education*. It concerned complaints about segregated schools from Black families in five other cities.

Thurgood Marshall, an African American lawyer, headed the NAACP's national legal team for this case. Many years later, in 1967, he became a Supreme Court justice himself—

Courtesy Library of Congress

NAACP lawyer Thurgood Marshall reading to his son, who grew up to be a lawyer.

the court's first Black justice. In his 1954 presentation to the court in *Brown v. Board of Education*, Marshall made the same basic point that Albion Tourgée had more than fifty years earlier in the *Plessy v. Ferguson* case: separating citizens based on race violates the 14th Amendment.

In addition, Marshall supported his argument by presenting the results of a research study by two prominent African American psychologists, Dr. Kenneth Clark and Dr. Mamie P. Clark, the first Black scholars to earn PhDs in psychology from Columbia University. Their research showed that living in a segregated society, where people are separated on the basis of skin color, could give Black youngsters a negative feeling about being Black and interfere with their performance in school. Seventy-seven years earlier, in 1877, Paul Trévigne had made a similar point in a lawsuit he filed to try to prevent the end of integrated schools in New Orleans (see Chapter 2). At that time, a judge rejected Trévigne's claim because there was no research to back up Trévigne's ideas. The research

BABY DOLLS MAKING HISTORY

In the research study that had such a powerful impact on the Supreme Court in the *Brown v. Board of Education* case, psychologists Dr. Kenneth and Dr. Mamie P. Clark presented four baby dolls to more than 250 African American children between the ages of three and seven. Just over half of the children were in Arkansas; the rest in Massachusetts. The dolls were identical except for skin color. Two dolls had brown skin with black hair and two had white skin with yellow hair. The Clarks asked the children such questions as which dolls were nice, which look bad, which they'd want to play with, and which were like them. A majority of the children preferred the white doll. Most said the brown doll "looks bad." There were no statistically significant differences between the responses of the Southern and Northern children. Some youngsters became upset at the end of the questioning when they had to choose which doll looked like them. This experiment seemed to show that living in a segregated society gave these children a negative feeling about being Black.

This doll was used by Dr. Kenneth Clark and Dr. Mamie P. Clark in their research study. Since 2015, it has been on display at the National Park Service's Brown v. Board of Education *National Historical Site in Topeka, Kansas. Behind the doll is a photo of a child who was shown two dolls during the study: one doll with brown skin and the other with white skin.*

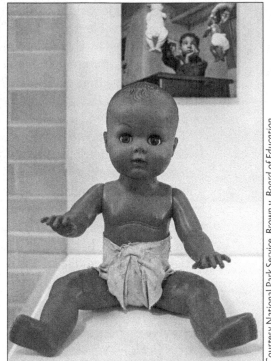

Courtesy National Park Service, Brown v. Board of Education National Historic Site

study that Thurgood Marshall cited in 1954 provided impressive evidence to support assertions that Trévigne and others had made about the impact of segregation on youngsters' self-esteem.

That research may have helped influence the court's nine justices (all white males) to see segregation from the point of view of a person of color. Chief Justice Earl Warren wrote the court's opinion. His comments showed that he was moved by the Clarks' research. In describing the impact of segregation on children of color, Warren wrote that:

> To separate them from others of similar age and qualifications solely because of their race generates a feeling of inferiority as to their status in the community that may affect their hearts and minds in a way unlikely ever to be undone.

All nine justices concluded that racially segregated schools were unconstitutional. In the statement announcing their decision, the justices noted that separating school children by race "denies to Negro children the equal protection of the laws guaranteed by the Fourteenth Amendment."

The court's statement also included a harsh criticism of the *Plessy v. Ferguson* decision: "The 'separate-but-equal' doctrine adopted in *Plessy v. Ferguson* . . . has no place in the field of public education."

The *Brown v. Board of Education* Supreme Court decision, issued in 1954, marked the beginning of the end of the Jim Crow era. But unjust rules and laws still existed, even in the education world. Louisiana and several other southern states refused for many years to integrate their schools. New Orleans didn't even begin to change its schools until 1960, and then did so only because of a firm order from Judge Skelly Wright, a federal judge in Louisiana. He delivered his order because of the school segregation lawsuit that A. P. Tureaud, Sr., had filed earlier.

Courtesy Jules Cahn Collection at the Historic New Orleans Collection, 1996.123.1.107xi

Leona Tate walking out of the McDonogh 19 Elementary School surrounded by the Federal Marshalls who accompanied her to and from school during the 1960 school year, protecting her from crowds of angry whites who opposed integration.

Judge Wright had been dealing with this lawsuit for several years, trying to make New Orleans desegregate its schools. In 1959, when the school board hadn't created a desegregation plan yet, he wrote a plan for them. It called for integrating gradually, starting with first graders. The school board tried to block that plan. But a higher federal court and then the U.S. Supreme Court refused to let the school board prevent integration. Even so, the school board put up so many obstacles that the first year of school desegregation in New Orleans in 1960 involved only two schools and just four African American girls, who were six years old.

That school year, armed U.S. Federal Marshals had to escort those brave girls to school each day to protect them from crowds of angry white people who shouted insults at the girls. Three of the Black girls—Leona Tate, Gail Etienne, and Tessie Prevost—spent first grade being taught in a classroom by themselves in a school that had no other students. White parents refused to send their children to this school. The fourth girl, Ruby Bridges, learned in a classroom all by herself in a different school. Three white families did send

---

DISSENT'S IMPACT

In preparing arguments to use at the Supreme Court in the 1954 *Brown v. Board of Education* case, Thurgood Marshall made use of ideas that Albion Tourgée had noted in his presentation to the court in the *Plessy v. Ferguson* case. Marshall also paid close attention to the comments that Justice John Harlan wrote in his statement dissenting from the majority opinion in the *Plessy v. Ferguson* decision. Thurgood Marshall is said to have found Harlan's eloquence inspiring and often re-read the Harlan dissent during his legal career, whenever his spirits needed lifting. "No opinion buoyed Marshall more in his pre-Brown days," recalled fellow NAACP lawyer Constance Baker Motley. "Marshall admired the courage of Harlan more than any justice who has ever sat on the Supreme Court. . . . Harlan was a solitary and lonely figure writing for posterity."

children to her school, but the white youngsters had separate classrooms from Ruby Bridges.

Phoebe Ferguson and Keith Plessy were only three years old in 1960. They didn't know what was going on at those two schools. Phoebe learned later that her mother had volunteered with a group called Save Our Schools that encouraged white families to accept integration and let children attend integrated schools. The official end to separate schools for white and Black students in New Orleans didn't happen until the 1970s. By then Keith and Phoebe were teenagers.

Sparking Protests

Even though the *Brown v. Board of Education* decision applied only to schools, it energized people to protest other kinds of injustice. One year after the *Brown* decision, Rosa Parks was arrested for refusing to move to the back of a bus in Montgomery, Alabama, in December 1955. Her arrest inspired the city's Black community to take part in a yearlong protest against bus segregation that was led by Rev. Dr. Martin Luther King, Jr. Thousands of Montgomery's Black residents boycotted the local bus company for a year and refused to ride its buses. They chose to walk to work or found ways to carpool, instead of paying to ride a bus. The boycott caused financial problems for the bus company.

The bus boycott continued until December 1956, when the U.S. Supreme Court ordered an end to segregation on any local buses in Montgomery. This order came in response to a lawsuit filed by the NAACP on behalf of five other Montgomery women who had refused to give up their seats on a bus or had been mistreated by a bus driver.

Over the next ten years, more protests against Jim Crow took place throughout the country. Lawyers kept filing anti-Jim Crow lawsuits, too. In 1958, A. P. Tureaud, Sr., won a court case that ended segregation on New Orleans buses and streetcars. The "race screen" signs that had divided Black and white riders became a thing of the past.

In 1960, sit-in protests started across the South, including in New Orleans. Protestors took seats at lunch counters that wouldn't serve Black customers. Sometimes these protestors

Courtesy Times-Picayune, September 9, 1960, Capital City Press/
Georges Media Group, Baton Rouge, LA, photo by Ralph Uribe

*A CORE (Congress of Racial Equality) protestor picketing in front of
a McCrory's store in New Orleans in 1960, urging people to boycott
the store because it didn't serve people of color at its lunch counter.*

were arrested, as happened in New Orleans, where college
students organized their own chapter of a new civil rights
organization that was leading these direct-action, non-violent
protests: CORE (the Congress of Racial Equality). This interracial group believed in the power of peaceful, non-violent
protest as a way to bring about change.

New Orleans CORE members held a boycott of many of
the city's stores, urging people not to shop at businesses that
wouldn't serve Black people at their lunch counters or wouldn't
hire them in responsible positions. These protests proved successful. As a result, some businesses opened their lunch counters to all and hired African Americans as sales clerks.

In early May 1961, college students from New Orleans and
elsewhere took part in a new kind of protest: CORE's Freedom Rides. They boarded buses that traveled throughout
the South to protest segregated bus stations and bus travel.
They were arrested when they broke Jim Crow rules about

PERSONAL PROTEST

"Long before I knew of Rosa Parks, my daddy took that screen and put it in the middle of the floor on the bus one day and told us to take our seat—and nothing happened," said Jerome Smith, speaking about the "race screen" that separated Black and white riders on New Orleans buses and streetcars. A few years later, when Jerome was about ten years old, he tried doing the same thing when he was by himself. This time, the driver threatened to call the police until an elderly Black woman stood up and "slapped me onside my head and told me, 'Don't disrespect white folks by trying to sit with them,'" Jerome recalled later. They got off and she quickly took him behind a nearby store. "She grabbed me and hugged me . . . and said she was proud of me." She added, "Don't stop." About ten years later, as a college student, he helped start the New Orleans chapter of CORE. He took part in protests at stores in New Orleans and then became one of the Freedom Riders. Several years later, he started an education program for youngsters in the Tremé section of New Orleans and gave Keith Plessy, age fifteen, his first job, as an art teacher in the program's summer camp. "Jerome Smith was a neighborhood hero," said Keith. "He was another who influenced me to seek my ancestor's history. He told me he considered Homer Plessy the first Freedom Rider."

what areas of a bus station a person of color could use. Reports about the arrest and mistreatment of the non-violent Freedom Riders appeared in newspapers and on TV screens across the nation and around the world. Jerome Smith, a New Orleans CORE member, was one of the Freedom Riders who was beaten severely. The news reports shocked the nation and embarrassed the federal government into taking action. By the end of May that year, the U.S. government issued strong regulations against racial discrimination on interstate transportation that would at last be enforced.

By the middle of 1963, segregation in state-to-state travel had mostly ended, on trains as well as on buses. By 1965, local transportation had dropped Jim Crow, too. What Homer

Protestors at the August 28, 1963, March on Washington for Jobs and Freedom.

Plessy and the Citizens' Committee had tried to accomplish more than seventy years earlier had finally happened.

In 1963, A. P. Tureaud, Sr., won another legal victory when a court ordered New Orleans to open all its public parks and playgrounds to people of all races. In August that same year, more than 200,000 people gathered in Washington, D.C., for the March on Washington for Jobs and Freedom, where Dr. King spoke about his dream of an America without segregation. That fall in New Orleans, thousands of African Americans and several hundred white supporters marched to City Hall to urge the mayor to speed up efforts to end segregation.

Protests and court cases around the nation finally persuaded the U.S. Congress to put an official end to the Jim Crow era with three new pieces of legislation:

- *The Civil Rights Act of 1964* prohibited discrimination on the basis of race, color, religion, sex, or national origin in public places or in employment; it required that any business serving the public had to be open to all.

- *The Voting Rights Act of 1965* sought to eliminate rules that made it hard for Black citizens to vote.
- *The Fair Housing Act of 1968* tried to address issues of discrimination in housing, but in many neighborhoods redlining had already caused severe economic damage that was hard to undo, as described in the previous chapter.

The Civil Rights Act of 1964 didn't suffer the same fate as a similar law in 1875 that had also outlawed discrimination in public places. In 1883, the U.S. Supreme Court overturned that 1875 law by claiming that the 14th Amendment only gave Congress the right to regulate the actions of states, not of businesses and individuals (as noted in Chapter 4). But

CHANGING AMERICA "OVER A BOWL OF GUMBO"

A restaurant in Tremé, one of New Orleans' main Black neighborhoods, played a part in the 1960s civil rights protests. Homer Plessy and members of the Citizens' Committee lived in Tremé in the 1890s, but this restaurant wasn't there then. Owned by Edgar (Dooky) Chase, Jr., with his wife, Leah Chase, as the master chef, Dooky Chase's Restaurant was a classy place where people of color could have special dinners and family celebrations at a time when Jim Crow kept them out of the city's fancy, whites-only eating places. Dooky Chase's was also a place where civil rights activists—Black and white—could meet to eat together and discuss plans. It began as a sandwich shop, but Leah Chase persuaded her husband to turn it into a fine restaurant that served gumbo seafood stew and other classic Louisiana specialties. She enjoyed feeding everyone, from Freedom Riders to NAACP leaders, including Thurgood Marshall. Later, she hosted two U.S. presidents: George W. Bush and Barack Obama. She liked to say, "We changed the course of America over a bowl of gumbo and some fried chicken." She told a *New York Times* reporter, "I just think that God pitches us a low, slow curve, but he doesn't want us to strike out. I think everything he throws at you is testing your strength, and you don't cry about it, and you go on."

those who wrote the 1964 Civil Rights Act didn't rely on the 14th Amendment for permission to create such a law. They cited a different part of the U.S. Constitution: the Commerce Clause. It appears at the start of the constitution, in Article 1. The Commerce Clause gives Congress the right "to regulate commerce with foreign nations, and among the several states."

Commerce "among the several states"—also known as interstate commerce—has to do with business dealings between states or between companies in different states. A whites-only motel in Georgia and a whites-only restaurant in Alabama challenged Congress's right to pass such a law. When this case reached the Supreme Court, the defenders of the 1964 Civil Rights Act were ready. They showed the court evidence that "discrimination by hotels and motels impedes interstate travel." They also showed that the Georgia motel and the Alabama restaurant participated in interstate commerce by advertising to out-of-state customers or by buying supplies from other states. The Supreme Court rejected those businesses' complaints and ruled in favor of the Civil Rights Act of 1964, declaring that it "is a valid exercise of Congress' power under the Commerce Clause."

Jim Crow Lingers On

It took a while for those new laws to weaken Jim Crow's hold everywhere. Many individuals found ways to continue treating people of color unfairly, despite what laws and courts said. For example, in 1958, the year after Keith Plessy and Phoebe Ferguson were born, a court ordered that City Park—one of New Orleans' largest parks—had to be open to people of color. But changes imposed by a court didn't always lead to Black people feeling welcome in a newly integrated space. A few years after the park was supposed to be open to all, Phoebe's African American babysitter wasn't allowed to ride with Phoebe on the carousel when they came to the park for what was supposed to be a fun outing (see Chapter 1).

Dr. Raynard Sanders, who later became a high school principal, recalled being treated badly as a youngster at City Park several years after the park officially desegregated. In 1961, he and other Black members of his Boy Scout troop entered the park. "It was my first trip into City Park, other than going to a football game," he explained. "We were just going to enjoy the facilities. We were not wanted. People there were cursing us out, calling us a bunch of racial slurs." He and his friends got the message and left.

The 1963 court victory that made segregation illegal at all of the city's other parks didn't wipe out the unofficial and often unwritten rules that continued to limit access, such as those at Keith's neighborhood park (described in Chapter 1). Those informal rules kept him from playing ball there on weekends when he was growing up.

Even such an impressive victory as the 1954 *Brown v. Board of Education* Supreme Court decision hasn't lived up to the hopes that many people had for it. Despite the official end to segregation in New Orleans and other school systems around the nation, there are many schools in both the North and the South, including in New Orleans, that don't have racially diverse student populations. Some schools appear to be just as segregated as when Jim Crow was running the show, although other schools are doing a good job of bringing people together. Jim Crow's grip has been hard to break. The damage it caused has lingered on.

New Orleans, like all U.S. cities, has big problems to solve. A prime example is the inequity revealed during the COVID-19 pandemic. A much higher percentage of African Americans in Louisiana died of COVID-19 compared to their representation in the state's population. The same was true in other states as well. The serious health conditions that burden people of color at higher rates than they do white people—such as heart disease, high blood pressure, and diabetes (as described in Chapter 6)—may have contributed to this tragic situation. The causes of the differences in illness levels and death rates faced by people of color in general, as well as during the COVID-19 crisis, need to be studied carefully to determine what kinds of changes New Orleans and the rest of the nation need to make.

But there have been advances, too, that mark a shift away from Jim Crow attitudes. In 1978, Ernest (Dutch) Morial became the first African American elected as mayor of New Orleans. Since then four other people of color have been elected mayor, serving for a total of more than thirty years so far. Another first occurred in 2018 when LaToya Cantrell became the first African American woman elected mayor of New Orleans. African Americans also serve as judges, as members of the New Orleans City Council, and in other official positions, including as chief justice of the Louisiana Supreme Court. Bernette Joshua Johnson has held that position since 2012, when she became the court's first African American chief justice. Another woman of color, Dr. Courtney Phillips, became the head of Louisiana's department of health in 2020.

These power shifts have led to other changes. Starting in the 1990s, many schools named for slaveholders received new names. The elementary school named for the 19th century

Courtesy Times-Picayune, October 3, 2008, Capital City Press/Georges Media Group, Baton Rouge, LA

This 2008 photo from the Times-Picayune *shows that by then the carousel in City Park in New Orleans welcomed children of color.*

free woman of color Marie Couvent was included in this name-changing because she too was a slaveholder. That school became the A. P. Tureaud Elementary School.

The 1990s also saw another building named for that famous civil rights lawyer: a classroom building at Louisiana State University. In 2011, this university also granted an honorary doctoral degree to Tureaud's son, A. P. Tureaud, Jr., who had been prevented from enrolling as an undergraduate at LSU more than fifty years before.

A major change in 2017 earned headlines around the nation. As a result of a vote by the New Orleans City Council, three statues of Confederate-era slaveholders were removed and taken away: statues of Confederate Generals Robert E. Lee and P. G. T. Beauregard, and of Jefferson Davis, the Confederacy's president. Also removed in 2017 was a monument about the 1874 Battle of Liberty Place, during which White League attackers killed eleven members of the city's integrated police force (described in Chapter 2).

Three years later, in 2020, the New Orleans City Council voted to create a commission to consider renaming streets, parks, and other public places that bear the names of slaveholders and Confederacy leaders and supporters. This vote came in response to protests that erupted in June 2020 in New Orleans and elsewhere around the nation in response to killings of unarmed African Americans by police. Perhaps these new protests will lead to a national examination of the persistence of Jim Crow attitudes and how to uproot them.

A different sign of change, however, has occurred in the neighborhood where Keith Plessy lived as a child. African American youngsters can now play at the neighborhood's St. Roch Park any day of the week. Children of color are also welcome to climb into the saddles of the horses and other animals on City Park's beautiful carousel and have fun circling round and round with all the other riders.

A "Reset"

When Phoebe and Keith learned as adults about the roles that their long-ago relatives played in creating—and also trying to prevent—the Jim Crow era and all the hardship that segregation caused, they decided to give new meanings to the words "Plessy" and "Ferguson." They didn't want their family names to be linked forever only to the unjust hoax of "separate-but-equal."

Courtesy Al Kennedy and Keith Plessy

Keith Plessy and members of his family attending a 1996 service at Homer Plessy's tomb in St. Louis Cemetery No. 1 in New Orleans to commemorate the 100th anniversary of the Plessy v. Ferguson *decision. Keith (in sunglasses, fourth from left, front row) is holding his daughter Kayla Marie Plessy, with his older daughter, Mia Lauren Plessy, standing next to him. Behind Mia is Marietta Plessy, the girls' mother and Keith's wife. Directly behind Keith stands his father, Paul Gustave Plessy. To the left of Kayla is Geraldine Talton, the cousin who had the photograph of Keith's great-grandfather that Keith used to make the drawing in Chapter 2. Leading the service and blessing the tomb is Father Jerome LeDoux (arms raised) of the St. Augustine Catholic Church, which Homer Plessy attended.*

DIGGING INTO
FAMILY ROOTS

"I didn't take it by the horns and find out everything about Homer Plessy," noted Keith Plessy, describing his reaction as a fifth grader to the news that he might be related to Homer Plessy. "I hated history," he admitted. "Every time the subject of history came up in class, I would draw pictures." That was partly because he loved to draw, and would later go to art school. His teachers realized that he was an artist at heart and would always ask him to do the holiday decorations for the classroom. But there was another reason history didn't grab his attention as a kid. He had a sense that he wasn't being told the whole story of what had really happened in the past. "The answers to questions I was trying to get as a kid were not in that history book in school. I guess I was more concerned about not being able to play in the park than I was in learning about my ancestors."

He became more interested in history in his twenties, after he graduated from art school in New Orleans. In 1979, his former elementary school, the Valena C. Jones Elementary School, asked him to decorate the walls inside the school with portraits of more than a hundred African American heroes. He painted pictures of Rev. Dr. Martin Luther King, Jr., and local New Orleans heroes, including civil rights lawyer A. P.

Tureaud, Sr. Keith spent about two years covering more than seventy-five percent of the school's walls with these portraits. In addition to political leaders, he also portrayed sports stars and musicians. Keith didn't paint a portrait of Homer Plessy, however, because there are no photos that show what he looked like.

"I was trying to express to kids that these are people who look like you. You can do what they can do," explained Keith. Teachers used the portraits as part of their lessons. They would have students write reports about the famous people who were looking at them from the school's walls. Then the teachers would post the student reports on the walls below the portraits.

Courtesy Al Kennedy, Keith Plessy, and Louisiana & Special Collections, University of New Orleans, from March 1980 issue of *Applause*, vol. 3, #9, pp. 1–2

● The Michelangelo of Jones

Continued from page 1

who, like Plessy, is a graduate of Jones. Historic and national figures are on the third floor.

As Plessy happily discovered, the portraits aren't just decoration. Teachers have begun to have their students write reports on the famous faces. The reports are posted below the portraits, and students get a lesson in history every time they walk through the halls.

Instead of bursting with pride at his already-monumental project, Plessy feels only the urgency to push himself farther and farther and to paint more and more. "I have at least 50 more portraits to paint before I will consider this job finished," he says.

One thing is certain, however, and that is the black history portrait collection will not be complete until a portrait of Keith Plessy adorns the walls of Jones Elementary.

ALLEN TOUSSAINT 1938–

FATS DOMINO 1928–

In his tribute to famous black Americans, local artist and former Jones student Keith Plessy did not neglect local music impressario Allen Toussaint and the legendary Fats Domino.

REV. DR. MARTIN LUTHER KING JR. 1929–1968

Keith Plessy with his portraits of Allen Toussaint and Fats Domino (top) that he painted on the walls of the Valena C. Jones Elementary School. These photos appeared in "Plessy Paints Pride: The Michelangelo of Jones," an article from Applause, *a 1980 Orleans Parish School Board publication. Here also is Keith's portrait in the school of Rev. Dr. Martin Luther King, Jr.*

When Keith was in his late thirties, his interest in history grew stronger. By then he was married with children, working as a bellman at a New Orleans hotel. In 1996, he met Keith Weldon Medley, an author who was starting to work on a book about Homer Plessy, *We as Freemen: Plessy v. Ferguson.* Medley had contacted as many members of the Plessy family as he could find and put Keith in touch with relatives he never knew he had, including a white cousin, Bobby Duplissey, who was also trying to learn about the family's past.

More recently, Keith Plessy connected with another cousin he hadn't known of before, Michael Nolden Henderson, who was also researching the family's history. Henderson wrote a book in 2013 on his findings, *Got Proof!* He spoke about his book on an episode of the PBS TV series *History Detectives,* sharing what he had learned about his family's past. "Michael does deep research," explained Keith. "He told me, 'When you start searching for your ancestors, you find they have been looking for you.'"

Keith Plessy is no longer a reluctant historian. "Now, I can't forget anything I hear about history. It has become a part of me," he observed. "What captivated me was the history of my ancestor." From the author of *We as Freemen,* Keith learned the real story behind Homer Plessy and the Citizens' Committee's long campaign against segregation and how that was connected to the unfair rules that puzzled him as a kid—fascinating facts that weren't in the history book at his elementary school.

When Keith heard that there would be a ceremony in New Orleans in May 1996 to commemorate the hundredth anniversary of the *Plessy v. Ferguson* Supreme Court decision, he and his wife and two young daughters became part of those gathering to mark this important milestone. The day's commemoration started at the St. Augustine Catholic Church in the Tremé neighborhood where Homer Plessy had lived. After prayers and singing at the church, everyone joined in a Second Line parade led by jazz musicians from the church to the cemetery where Homer Plessy is buried, St. Louis Cemetery No. 1. Second Line jazz parades are a tradition in New Orleans funerals. The ceremony and parade provided Homer Plessy with the kind of celebratory funeral that didn't happen

Courtesy Al Kennedy and Keith Plessy

The Second Line parade that went from the St. Augustine Catholic Church in Tremé to Homer Plessy's tomb in St. Louis Cemetery No. 1, as part of the 1996 ceremony honoring Homer Plessy.

after his death in 1925. "We marched and set his soul free," said Keith.

Keith also learned from Medley, the *We as Freemen* author, about the first two members of the Plessy family to come to America: Germain Plessy and Dominique Plessy, two white men who were born in Bordeaux, France. They arrived in Louisiana in the early 1800s, after escaping from Haiti, where they had been living. They were among the many French people who fled from what had been a French colony after Toussaint L'Ouverture led a slave rebellion that ended French control there and established Haiti as an independent country.

Keith is descended from Germain Plessy, a merchant who decided to stay in New Orleans. He and a free woman of color named Catherina Mathieu, also called Catiche, lived as husband and wife. Her mother was Agnes, the enslaved woman described in Chapter 2 who gained her freedom in 1779. A law against interracial marriage meant that Catiche and Germain couldn't legally marry, but together they had eight children, all of whom used Plessy as a last name.

SEARCHING FOR FREEDOM

Keith Plessy's cousin, Michael Nolden Henderson, began his family history research by looking for relatives with the last name of Mathieu, his grandmother's name before she married. An elderly cousin, Leonor Douroux Lombard, could remember family stories that reached back more than two hundred years to the first relative to use Mathieu as a last name: Homer Plessy's great-grandmother, Agnes Ramis. After Agnes gained her freedom in 1779, she called herself Marie Agnes *Mathieu* Ramis. She also used Mathieu as a last name for her seven children. Cousin Leonor had heard that those children's father was Mathieu Devaux, but that the children always said, "They wouldn't allow us to use Daddy's last name." Because mixed-race marriages were illegal, Agnes couldn't officially use the last name Devaux. So she started a new family line by using her partner's first name as a last name, "providing her and her children a connection to Mathieu Devaux," wrote Michael Henderson in his book, *Got Proof!* Devaux left all his wealth to these children after he died. "Knowing that Mathieu and Agnes had managed to overcome legal limitations, maintain a longstanding relationship, and produce a thriving family made me proud," said Henderson. Now, he is trying to find which slave ship brought Agnes's great-grandparents from Africa to Louisiana. He was surprised to learn that Mathieu Devaux fought in a militia commanded by Louisiana's Spanish governor, Bernardo de Galvez, to help America win its freedom from Britain during the American Revolution.

One of Catiche and Germain's eight children was Homer Plessy's father. Another was Homer's uncle, whose son was Homer's cousin. This cousin became Keith Plessy's great-grandfather. (The Family Trees section at the end of the book can help make this family history a little clearer.)

As for Keith's cousin, Michael Nolden Henderson, the family historian, he is descended from a brother of Catiche. Henderson found that Germain Plessy bought and sold people who were enslaved but hasn't seen any records showing that Catiche herself bought any enslaved people.

Germain Plessy's relationship with Catiche caused a split with the other Plessy who came to New Orleans with him, Dominique Plessy. Dominique married a white woman and moved with her to an area north of New Orleans. Dominique and his wife didn't want to have anything to do with Germain and Catiche's mixed-race family. The white branch of the family later changed their last name to Duplissey.

"Racism within the family caused us to separate for 200 years," noted Keith. Now the two parts of the family are back in touch, working together to track down more Plessy relatives, thanks to author Keith Weldon Medley and the book he wrote.

That author also brought Keith Plessy together with Phoebe Ferguson.

Phoebe's Discovery

When Phoebe Ferguson's fifth grade class in California began studying the *Plessy v. Ferguson* Supreme Court case, she thought, "I'm from New Orleans. I have that name." But she didn't explore further. Phoebe was more interested in art than in tracking down family history, just as Keith was when he

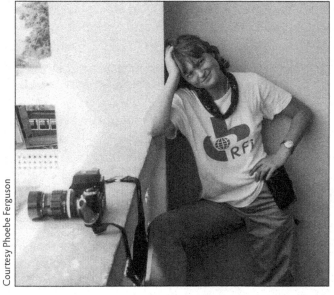

Courtesy Phoebe Ferguson

Phoebe Ferguson in Somalia in 1981, when she was in her mid-20s, working as a photographer for a foundation that was documenting art and culture in Somalia, for a project on cross-cultural understanding.

was a child. She went to art school, became a photographer, got married, moved to New York City, and lived in a multi-racial Brooklyn neighborhood where she raised her children and worked as a photographer for advertising agencies. In her forties, she wanted to do something more creative. Her marriage had ended, and her kids were grown. She went back to school to learn how to make documentary films.

She decided to make a film about the Mardi Gras celebrations in New Orleans. As a little girl, Phoebe had always enjoyed the parades and fancy-dress balls of Mardi Gras. It seemed like a good idea for her first film-making production. Mardi Gras occurs every year before Ash Wednesday, the day that marks the start of Lent. During Lent, which lasts the six weeks from Ash Wednesday to Easter Sunday, many Christians give up certain foods. At the huge celebrations in New Orleans on the Tuesday before Lent begins, people let loose. They parade, sing, dance, and eat the special treats that they will give up during Lent. This day of over-the-top festivities is called "Mardi Gras," which in French means "Fat Tuesday." (In French, "mardi" is Tuesday and "gras" means fat.)

Phoebe traveled to New Orleans in early 2002 to do some filming at the Zulu Ball, one of the big parties held by Mardi Gras social clubs. On this first trip back after a long absence, Phoebe said, "I got off the plane and felt this enormous feeling of oppression, and not just because of the humidity." By then, she was well-aware of the civil rights history of New Orleans and of the country in general. As she stepped off that plane and began to re-connect with her hometown, "I had this fear in my stomach, about knowing that the old-line white legacy still existed there and that those people were part of my parents' community, and of the Mardi Gras world. Both sides of our family were involved in Mardi Gras, my mother's side and the Ferguson side. A good deal of the people who started Mardi Gras in the 1850s were part of the generation of white people who wanted to regain their power after the Civil War."

She hoped her film would show different aspects of Mardi Gras. The Zulu Ball was a good place to start. It is hosted by a social club with mainly African American members, and Phoebe had never been to this ball before. At Mardi Gras balls, some people dress up like kings and queens. The man helping Phoebe with the filming brought her over to meet one of the Zulu Ball's queens, who was standing on a platform. Phoebe looked up, and there was Minnie Lou Williams, her childhood babysitter. "She looked at me and said, 'Phoebe?'"

After the Zulu Ball, Phoebe and her former babysitter got together to talk about all that had happened to them since Phoebe left New Orleans at age ten, after her father died. "Minnie told me, 'Your mother put me through college. I became a teacher.' I never knew that," said Phoebe. "That opened up a whole other part of the film." Phoebe had planned to do a film that would include white Mardi Gras parades and social clubs. Instead, her film, *Member of the Club*, focused on the Mardi Gras celebrations of people of color. Her film tells the story of one family's participation in Mardi Gras balls sponsored by the Original Illinois Club. Founded in 1895, it was the first African American social club to participate in Mardi Gras. "That was my re-entry into New Orleans, making that film. But because of the film, I got disowned by my godfather. When he found out I did a film about the Black community in New Orleans, he never talked to me again. That shows how people who were raised here in the generation after the *Plessy* decision were never able to let go of their prejudices, not even fifty years after the *Brown v. Board of Education* decision."

On another visit to the city to attend the funeral for her family's former housekeeper, Georgia Lee Kearny, some of Phoebe's Louisiana relatives warned her not to attend the service. They feared it was too dangerous to go to the church in Ms. Kearny's neighborhood. A taxi driver even asked her if she was sure she wanted to go there. "I said, 'I'm really sure. Will you please just take me there.' I was the only white person in the church. I walked down the aisle to where the family was and I remember them holding my hand throughout the whole ceremony. I'm thinking, 'Really? This is where that guy was afraid to take me? In this incredibly loving, accepting community.'"

In late 2002, when she was back in New York, Phoebe had another surprise. She received a phone call from a man who asked if she was the great-great-granddaughter of John Howard Ferguson. The caller had just bought the judge's old house in New Orleans and wanted to fix it up the way it was when

The cover of the DVD of Phoebe Ferguson's documentary film, Member of the Club, *which came out in 2008.*

Courtesy Phoebe Ferguson

the judge lived there. He said he was calling people named Ferguson to try to find a relative who might know about the judge's house. By chance, Phoebe's sister had just sent her a box of old family papers. In the box was an envelope Phoebe hadn't opened yet. It was supposed to contain documents listing members of the Ferguson family going back many years.

"While I was on the phone," Phoebe recalled, "I ripped open the envelope and ran my finger down the page. There it was: John Howard Ferguson." He was indeed her great-great-grandfather.

Courtesy Keith Plessy and Phoebe Ferguson

Keith Plessy and Phoebe Ferguson around the time that they first met, in 2004.

IT'S PLESSY AND FERGUSON NOW

"I started investigating immediately," said Phoebe, after learning from family documents that her great-great-grandfather was John Howard Ferguson, the judge who had ruled against Homer Plessy in 1892. Phoebe's mother had died several years earlier and wasn't there to answer the new questions Phoebe now had about her family's history. Her sister didn't know that part of the family's history, either. So Phoebe traveled to New Orleans to see what she could discover.

She contacted the law library, hoping to find information that could help her understand why John Howard Ferguson had ruled against Homer Plessy. "I was looking for personal papers. I never found them. There don't seem to be any," she explained.

Someone at the law library told her about a new book on Homer Plessy, *We as Freemen*, that might answer her questions—the book by Keith Weldon Medley that had already helped Keith Plessy learn about his family history. Phoebe phoned the author. He invited her to come to a book signing for *We as Freemen* at a New Orleans historical society.

When she arrived, the author said to her, "There is somebody I want you to meet."

Courtesy Pelican Publishing

The book that brought the two families together.

A tall man walked over and said, "Hi, I'm Keith Plessy."

"I'm Phoebe Ferguson," said Phoebe. She was astonished to meet someone named Plessy. She was also deeply embarrassed about her family's role in starting Jim Crow. So Phoebe blurted out, "Oh, my God, I'm so sorry."

Keith Plessy laughed and said, "It's no longer *Plessy v. Ferguson*. It's Plessy *and* Ferguson. You weren't alive during that time. I wasn't either. It's time for us to change that whole image."

"He invited me to lunch with his family the next day," said Phoebe.

"We had a big New Orleans dinner," Keith explained, "with gumbo, bread pudding, and potato salad. Keith Weldon Medley came along. My wife was there. I met Phoebe's family later."

"When I went back to New York," recalled Phoebe, "and told people that I had met him, they were so astounded. They said, 'How could you possibly be friends?' Keith Plessy got the same reaction." People couldn't understand why he wasn't angry with someone from Judge John Howard Ferguson's family.

"It was my mother's influence," Keith explained, "her strictness in not hating people. Hate was not allowed in our house. Learn to love people. And if you don't love them, accept them the way they are and move on with your life."

Besides, as Keith noted, Judge Ferguson might have had a reason for his court decision that had nothing to do with the 14th Amendment. Keith had learned from the book *We as Freemen* that in 1891—a year before Homer Plessy's arrest and also a year before John Howard Ferguson became a judge—a mob of white men in New Orleans lynched eleven white men with Italian last names. Those eleven men had just been found *not* guilty of killing the local police chief, but the white mob didn't like the court's decision. Members of the mob broke into the prison where the eleven men were held, shot them, and then dragged these prisoners outside to lynch them by hanging them from light posts or trees, and then shooting them again. The Ku Klux Klan and other white supremacist groups had used lynching for many years to attack anyone who stood in their way, whether they were Black or white, immigrants, or any other group. The Equal Justice Initiative estimates that during Reconstruction, from 1865 to 1876, more than 2,000 lynchings of Black men, women, and children took place, primarily in southern states, with over 700 occurring in Louisiana. From the end of Reconstruction to 1950, there were an additional 4,084 racial terror lynchings in the South. Louisiana had one of the highest rates of these murders.

The lynch mob that killed those Italian immigrants included lawyers, newspaper editors, and other important members of white New Orleans society. This lynching made national news and was applauded by the *New York Times*, which seemed to have shared the prejudice that many white people felt toward immigrants at that time.

What if Judge Ferguson made a court ruling that this mob of well-connected people didn't like? "It wouldn't take much for him to be hanging from a rope or shot in the head," noted Keith. "The violence could go in different directions. If you stood in the way of the system, you could be killed. Back then, people 'disappeared.' Matter of fact, the judge that sat on the bench just before him 'disappeared' under mysterious circumstances right before Judge Ferguson was appointed. You never know what situation he was forced to deal with."

No matter what Judge Ferguson's reasons might have been for his decision, Keith said, "My mother's influence was enough that when I met Phoebe, I understood that what happened in 1892 and 1896 was none of her doing. I saw her as a person. She saw me in exactly the same way. We became friends almost instantly."

Changing the Story

Keith and Phoebe got together whenever she came to New Orleans from New York to work on her film. Then in 2005, Hurricane Katrina struck, causing widespread flooding, death, and destruction in New Orleans. The storm destroyed the homes of people who were featured in Phoebe's film. The storm damaged Keith's home, too, and his old elementary school, which still had the portraits of African American heroes that he had painted on the school's walls about twenty-five years earlier. Keith and his family moved to Memphis for a year until he could repair his house.

Phoebe was in New York during Katrina but couldn't stand being away from the people she had come to know in New Orleans who were suffering. She packed a truck with supplies for them and drove it to New Orleans. Not long after, she moved back home to New Orleans. She has been living there ever since.

"We stayed in touch all through the whole ordeal of Katrina," said Keith. "Had I not met Phoebe Ferguson before Katrina, I might have stayed in Memphis. I was doing great in Memphis. But my wife and my daughters cried every day to

Courtesy Keith Plessy, photos by Phoebe Ferguson

Keith Plessy had a chance to visit inside the Valena C. Jones School building several years after it was damaged by Hurricane Katrina. Standing in the building's ruined hallways, he examined the images he painted about Rev. Dr. Martin Luther King, Jr., and used a flashlight to see what was left of his Thurgood Marshall portrait.

come back here. All the women who meant something to me in my life wanted to come back to New Orleans. So I came back."

Phoebe began volunteering in New Orleans for the Amistad Research Center, which focuses on the history of slavery, race relations, African American communities, and the civil rights movement. Phoebe now lives near Keith and his family in New Orleans, and not far from the old house where Judge Ferguson lived.

In 2007, Phoebe, Keith, and Keith's brother attended the opening of an exhibit about *Plessy v. Ferguson* at the Louisiana Supreme Court building in New Orleans. A photo of them together at this exhibit appeared on the front page of the local newspaper. "We were so blown away by how people responded to the knowledge of us getting together. Our being together was a powerful symbol of 'coming together,' a kind of national reconciliation," explained Phoebe. Maybe the "coming together" of their two families could help others reach out and connect with people from different backgrounds, too.

They spoke about these ideas with friends who were interested in New Orleans history, including author Keith Weldon Medley; A. P. Tureaud, Jr., the son of the NAACP lawyer; and Rev. Brenda B. Square, at that time the archivist at the Amistad Research Center in New Orleans.

"We decided to create the Plessy and Ferguson Foundation to teach the history of the case and why it's still relevant today," noted Phoebe. She and Keith Plessy, along with Keith Weldon Medley and Rev. Square became the official founders of the Plessy and Ferguson Foundation. They continue to work together on its various projects. "Our goal," explained Phoebe, "is to keep the history of the case alive, keep the story of the struggle alive, and the importance of fighting for your rights."

Keith added, "Our foundation is a 'flip on the script.' As opposed to Plessy 'versus' Ferguson, we are Plessy 'and' Ferguson."

They chose to begin the work of the foundation at the place where the *Plessy v. Ferguson* case started in 1892—at the street corner where the detective hired by the Citizens' Committee pulled Homer Plessy off an East Louisiana Railroad train and arrested him for daring to break the law and sit in a car for white passengers.

THEIR TIME HAD COME

After the *Plessy v. Ferguson* decision in 1896, Rodolphe Desdunes continued to write, although not for *The Crusader* newspaper. It had stopped publication after the court decision. He worked as a customs inspector and in his spare time wrote a book published in 1911—*Our People and Our History*. It tells of notable members of the New Orleans Creole community, including Louis Martinet and Aristide Mary. The book describes the short-lived Unification Movement of 1873, which brought white and Black people together to try to end racial discrimination. In describing the Unification Movement in his book, Desdunes wrote: "The movement failed, but we have retained the memory of it. If it did not succeed, it was because it was premature." The Plessy and Ferguson Foundation hopes to show that for the ideals championed by the Unification Movement, their time may at last have come.

Times-Picayune, February 11, 2009, Capital City Press/Georges Media Group, Baton Rouge, LA, photo by Ted Jackson

In 2009, this photo of Phoebe and Keith appeared in the Times-Picayune *newspaper, just before the Plessy and Ferguson Foundation launched its first project. They are standing on the train tracks near where Homer Plessy was arrested in 1892.*

Courtesy Phoebe Ferguson

Members of the Plessy and Ferguson families gathered in February 2009 for the dedication of the Plessy and Ferguson Foundation's first historical marker. Front row (left to right): *Kayla Marie Plessy (Keith's daughter), Noël Anderson (Phoebe's daughter), and Judge Michael Bagneris.* Back row (left to right): *Keith Plessy, Marietta Plessy (Keith's wife), Geraldine Talton (cousin of Keith's father), Paul Gustave Plessy (Keith's father), Vivian Plessy (Keith's stepmother), Stephen Plessy (Keith's cousin).*

COMING TOGETHER

"Because of the mystery that was present when I was a kid, trying to get answers to questions that were not in books, I saw my purpose was to eliminate that for the next generation," said Keith Plessy. "Gather the right information through research and put it out there. Make it available to people at all times."

Trained as visual artists, Keith and Phoebe found a visual way to provide information on the history of the Plessy case and on other civil rights events. They decided to install historical markers—large metal plaques with fascinating information on both sides. These markers tell stories of "African American resistance and achievement around the city," explained Phoebe. "The plaques are a form of public art." They deliver history "on the go," surprising people as they walk down a street. As Keith noted, "You walk up on it and it's right there."

"Placing historical markers in New Orleans about civil rights history had long been Keith Weldon Medley's dream," said Phoebe, about the author who introduced Keith and Phoebe to their families' history and to each other. "He had made a list of markers he wanted to create long before we came on the scene. We just helped make it happen."

Keith, Phoebe, and their supporters spent a year planning their first marker. By chance, the arts program that Keith had attended during high school, the New Orleans Center for Creative Arts (NOCCA), had moved to Press Street, not far from where Homer Plessy boarded the train for his short, history-making train ride. No longer a part-day arts program, as it was when Keith was a teenager, NOCCA became a full-day conservatory of the arts, open to high school students from across Louisiana.

The depot where Homer Plessy boarded the train in June 1892 is no longer there. It was located at the edge of what is now the NOCCA parking lot. Homer Plessy's train traveled only about a block farther down Press Street before stopping at the intersection with Royal Street. That's where the detective hired by the Citizens' Committee pulled Plessy out of the car for white passengers and made the arrest.

Officials from NOCCA and other local community groups, including the Crescent City Peace Alliance, helped Keith and Phoebe plan the marker. Near the corner where the arrest occurred, the school's non-profit partner, the NOCCA Institute, owns a small grassy park that was already known as Plessy Park.

Local activists and educators had been working for several years to try to turn that little plot of land near the train tracks into a park celebrating Homer Plessy and New Orleans civil rights history. Award-winning New Orleans sculptor, the late John T. Scott, had drawn up plans in 2004 for the completed park. A central element was to have been a steel railroad track along which there could be information about episodes in African American history. Among those working on this project were members of the Crescent City Peace Alliance and the Douglass Community Coalition, as well as educators from the nearby Frederick Douglass High School and leaders of the school's Students at the Center writing program. These groups had held celebrations at Plessy Park in 2004 and 2005.

But when Hurricane Katrina struck in August 2005, it derailed the plans for developing Plessy Park. Artist John Scott had fled to Houston in advance of Katrina. Flood waters and the following chaos in New Orleans damaged his studio and many of his sculptures. He died in Houston two years later.

Much changed in New Orleans after Katrina, as the city struggled to recover from the devastation of the storm. By

Plessy Park, where the Plessy and Ferguson Foundation's first marker is located.

Photo by Amy Nathan

2009, the NOCCA Institute had acquired Plessy Park and agreed to let the Plessy and Ferguson Foundation install its first historical marker at the park's edge, near the intersection where Homer Plessy's arrest occurred.

Author Keith Weldon Medley wrote the text for the sturdy metal historical marker. One side of the marker provides information about the Citizens' Committee campaign and the ultimate success of its legal arguments nearly sixty years later with the *Brown v. Board of Education* decision. The other side of the marker tells a little about Homer Plessy and Judge Ferguson and also lists the names of all the members of the Citizens' Committee who worked so hard to try to overturn the Separate Car Act.

Keith and Phoebe chose a special day to unveil the marker and announce the creation of the Plessy and Ferguson Foundation—February 12, 2009. It was the 200th anniversary of the birth of Abraham Lincoln and the 100th anniversary of the founding of the NAACP. It was also Keith Weldon Medley's birthday and a few weeks after the inauguration of the nation's first African American president, Barack Obama.

Photo by Amy Nathan

"Unfortunately I was hit by a truck on my motorcycle the night before and was in a hospital," said Phoebe. She missed the unveiling ceremony. Keith's daughter Kayla Marie Plessy and Noël Anderson, Phoebe's daughter, unveiled the plaque together. "Then Phoebe's daughter and I announced the formation of the Plessy and Ferguson Foundation," explained Keith.

Nine years later, in 2018, the Plessy and Ferguson Foundation persuaded government officials to change the name for the stretch of Press Street that runs from the NOCCA parking lot to the corner where the historical marker stands. That section of Press Street is now called Homer Plessy Way.

Also in 2018, the NOCCA Institute commissioned Ayo Scott, a local artist and the son of sculptor John T. Scott, to paint a mural on a wall along one side of Plessy Park that would show scenes connected to the *Plessy v. Ferguson* story. The title that Ayo Scott chose for this artwork—"'These Are Times': The Legacy of Homer Plessy"—comes from a poem by New Orleans spoken-word poet Kataalyst Alcindor. A few panels from the mural have already been pictured in earlier chapters of this book. Here is an excerpt from a description of the mural on Ayo Scott's website:

> This mural celebrates the everyday man who chooses to stand up and fight for civil and human rights. It is a series of vignettes that show pieces of the struggles of civil rights in America, the accomplishments of past activism, and visions of an ideal future. The center-piece of the mural is a blindfolded black boy who is holding the scales of justice next to a dancing black boy dressed as Liberty, asking the question of the viewer what might liberty and justice look like through the eyes of another person.

The mural's last panel includes the statement the Citizens' Committee made in their final report on the efforts to overturn the Separate Car Act: "We, as freemen, still believe that we were right and our cause is sacred." The artist expanded on the quote, as seen in this photo, so that it encompasses

An image from the mural that Ayo Scott created for Plessy Park.

Courtesy Ayo Scott, photo by Amy Nathan

Ayo Scott's title for his mural in Plessy Park comes from a poem by New Orleans spoken-word poet Kataalyst Alcindor. In the mural, the poem is printed on the shirt of a blind-folded young man (see Chapter 5 and the book's cover). Here is the poem:

"These Are Times" by Kataalyst Alcindor

And the white man says
"These are dark times"
And the dark man says
"These are times"
And the woman says
"Are they?"
And we must all say
"Yes"

women as well as men. He added the words "FREE PEO-PLE" under the word "FREEMEN." The artist emphasized the role of women even more by placing that quote on the shirt of Dodie Smith-Simmons, a well-known New Orleans civil rights activist who took part in the 1961 Freedom Rides.

More Markers

Keith Plessy serves as president of the Plessy and Ferguson Foundation, and Phoebe Ferguson is the executive director. The foundation's board of directors includes members of both families, as well as New Orleans educators, civil rights activists, and artists. In choosing events to highlight with additional historical markers, the foundation partners with local organizations.

"When we're about to put up a marker, we make the neighborhood aware and seek their input," Keith explained. "We do a ceremony for the unveiling of the marker. At the ceremony, we have a community that comes together. Word gets out to other neighborhoods, and they say, 'Wait a minute. We have something that happened here.' They give us a list. You have people who have been wanting to do this for so long, and when they see it happen, they say, 'We can do that, too.' It's rewarding to see people wanting to learn more rather than leaving legacy behind."

Rev. Brenda B. Square, a board member of the foundation, is the director of its Historical Marker Projects. As a former archivist at the Amistad Center, she said she "came to see the many stories that have not been recorded in our history books as vital. I see our historic sites as sacred spaces. They embody stories which chronicle a history of ongoing struggle, stories which also illuminate today's issues. If we can unite the forces that have divided our communities and bring reconciliation, healing, and equity, we will break through the division and hostility that cripple our nation and work together to build a better future."

In addition to the one in Plessy Park, the Plessy and Ferguson Foundation has installed four other historical markers. The following sections describe the four additional markers that had been installed by the end of 2019. It plans to create a new marker focusing on the 1960s civil rights protests in New Orleans, and another one at Dooky Chase's Restaurant to honor its role in those protests and in the life of the community. Keith Weldon Medley wrote the text for all the markers except the one about Straight University. (See the Historical Markers section at the end of the book for photos of the text on each of the foundation's markers.)

- *The McDonogh 19 Elementary School Marker:* This marker celebrates the courage of Leona Tate, Gail Etienne, and Tessie Prevost. They made history as six-year-olds when they integrated the McDonogh 19 Elementary School in 1960. On November 14, 2010—exactly fifty years after the day they first entered that school as children—all three attended the unveiling of the historical marker in front of the school building. Also attending the ceremony were the Federal Marshalls who had protected them each day during that school year. Leona Tate helped create this historical marker. The building is no longer used as a school, but is listed on the National Register of Historic Places, so it can never be torn down. In 2020, ten years after the

Courtesy Phoebe Ferguson

*At the center of this photo of the unveiling of the historical marker
at the McDonogh 19 Elementary School are the three women who,
as six-year-olds, integrated the school in 1960: (left to right) Gail
Etienne, Tessie Prevost, and Leona Tate, with her grandchildren,
Cornelius Cooper, Jr., and Beatrice Bartholomew. The man on
the far left of the photo and the two men on the far right were
the Federal Marshalls who escorted the girls to school each
day that school year. The man standing next to Gail Etienne is
A. P. Tureaud, Jr.*

installation of the historical marker, Leona Tate's Foundation, in partnership with Alembic Community Development, purchased the building. Now known as the
Tate Etienne Prevost Interpretive Center, it will include
a museum and twenty-five affordable housing units for
seniors. The Center will also offer antiracism training,
taught by the People's Institute for Survival and Beyond to
help change attitudes and bring people together. The other
New Orleans school integrated in 1960, by six-year-old
Ruby Bridges, is still used as a school, with a statue in its
courtyard of a young Ruby Bridges. The motto of her Ruby
Bridges Foundation is: "Racism is a grown-up disease and
we must stop using our children to spread it."

- *The Valena C. Jones Elementary School Marker:* In 2015, in
  coordination with Beecher Memorial Congregational
  United Church of Christ and the Orleans Parish School
  Board, the Plessy and Ferguson Foundation installed a
  marker to honor the Valena C. Jones Elementary School.
  It was the first public school for children of color in the
  7th Ward area of New Orleans. In 1911, a Black community group, with support from Beecher Memorial Church,
  rented a building to start this school after the city's school
  board failed to provide one in that area for children of
  color. After a 1915 hurricane destroyed the rented building, the community group persuaded the school board to
  construct a new building for the school on four lots the
  community had bought for that purpose. It opened in 1916.
  Community leaders, including civil rights lawyer A. P.
  Tureaud, Sr., later started a campaign to create a larger
  building to accommodate the school's growing student
  body. It opened in 1929. Some famous graduates are Dutch
  Morial (elected New Orleans' first Black mayor in 1978),
  Andrew Young (former mayor of Atlanta and U.S. ambas-
  sador to the United Nations), A. P. Tureaud, Jr. (educator),
  and Keith Plessy, who decorated the school's walls in the
  late 1970s with portraits of African American heroes.

  The school closed in 2005 when the state government
  took over the city's schools after Hurricane Katrina. Officials wanted to sell the building, which might have led to it
  being torn down. But the Plessy and Ferguson Foundation
  persuaded the city to save the school because of its historic
  importance. Rev. Square explained why: "We consider
  Jones School a sacred space with a sacred legacy, which was
  a gift for the children of the 7th Ward. There was a dental
  program, a health program and they fed the kids. Pioneering efforts grew out of that school." Keith added, "We want
  eventually to have a developer build something inside the
  building that deals with education, health, and wellness—
  a lifeline for the community." The school's name illustrates
  its historic significance. Valena C. Jones, a role model for
  the community, taught in the city's schools for children of
  color in the late 1800s. She was voted the "most popular
  African-American teacher in the city." She had to retire in

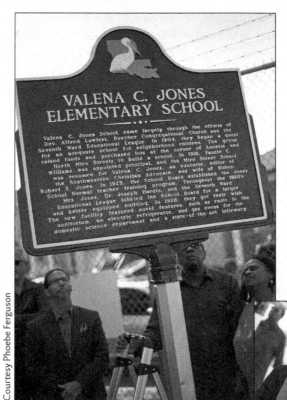

Keith Plessy (left) watching the unveiling of the Valena C. Jones Elementary School historical marker.

Rev. Brenda B. Square (below) speaking at the unveiling ceremony.

Courtesy Phoebe Ferguson

Courtesy Rev. Brenda B. Square

Courtesy the Charles L. Franck Studio Collection at The Historic New Orleans Collection, 1979.325.1846

The Valena C. Jones Elementary School's building that was dedicated in 1929.

1901 when she married, because married women weren't allowed to work as teachers. She then helped edit a local newspaper with her husband. Shortly after her death in 1917, officials named the school in her honor.

- *The Pythian Temple Marker:* A marker installed in 2017 celebrates the achievement of Smith W. Green, an African American self-made millionaire. In 1908, he built a seven-story building to house the headquarters of the Grand Lodge, Colored Order of the Knights of Pythias of Louisiana, an organization he led. Founded in 1864, the Knights of Pythias were supposed to bring people together after the Civil War, but after Reconstruction ended, white segregationists rejected Black members. So African Americans formed their own Pythian groups. Designed by a top architectural firm in New Orleans, the Pythian Temple won praise from a major architecture magazine and even from a local white-owned newspaper, the *Times-Picayune*, which called it "the biggest business enterprise ever attempted by the colored race in the United States."

  Born into slavery, Green became wealthy, first as a grocer and then as the owner of a company that sold insurance to Black customers at a time when other companies wouldn't. His insurance company had offices in the building, as did other Black-owned businesses and the local branch of the NAACP. Homer Plessy worked as a salesman for an insurance company in the building. With a theater and rooftop garden where jazz artists performed, including trumpeter Louis Armstrong, the Pythian Temple was a stylish place where people of color could socialize and feel respected during the Jim Crow era. "Outside the doors of the building, they were regarded as second-class citizens," observed Will Bradshaw, who bought the building in 2015. By then it had become rundown and stood empty. The Pythians lost ownership of it in 1941, for financial reasons. New owners hid its beautiful brick exterior behind an unattractive metal covering. Bradshaw's company restored the building to its former glory. The historical marker, located across the street, displays a photo of the original building. "People can read the plaque and look across the street to see that it has been restored to the way

Courtesy Phoebe Ferguson, photos by Abdul Aziz

At the unveiling of the Pythian Temple historical marker are (left to right): A.P. Tureaud, Jr., Keith Weldon Medley, Judy Geddes Bajoie (a great-great granddaughter of George G. Geddes, a member of the Citizens' Committee), Keith Plessy, Phoebe Ferguson, Rev. Brenda B. Square, Dr. Raynard Sanders, and Dodie Smith-Simmons.

it was in 1908," explained Phoebe. Keith is working with the new owners to have murals placed in the building that depict Green and others who reflect the building's spirit.

• *The Straight University Marker:* The Homer Plessy story also has a connection to a marker installed in 2019 on Esplanade Avenue's grassy median strip—or "neutral ground," as it's called in New Orleans. The marker stands near the original location of Straight University. In 1876, Louis

Martinet, *The Crusader* newspaper's founder and member of the Citizens' Committee, was the first graduate of Straight University's law school. The American Missionary Association had founded this university in 1869 to provide higher education for African Americans after the Civil War. The first university for people of color in the city, it trained many of the lawyers, educators, clergy, and others who would lead the struggle for equal rights. The marker's text, written by Rev. Square and the Preservation Resource Center, notes that in 1877, when U.S. troops left the city at the end of Reconstruction, the university's main building was destroyed by fire: "set ablaze in an act of arson." The school moved to another building and later joined with New Orleans University in 1930 to become Dillard University. Other graduates with a link to the Homer Plessy story include Rodolphe Desdunes, *The Crusader* writer, and P. B. S. Pinchback, Louisiana's first African American gov-

At the unveiling of the Straight University historical marker are (left to right): Dr. Raynard Sanders, Dr. Megan Holt, Rev. Brenda B. Square, Phoebe Ferguson, and Keith Plessy.

ernor. Two graduates have a connection to Keith Plessy: Fannie C. Williams, a principal of his elementary school, and Valena C. Jones, the educator for whom that school was named.

Plessy Day

Besides creating historical markers, the Plessy and Ferguson Foundation hosts programs every year on Homer Plessy Day—June 7th—the day in 1892 when Homer Plessy was arrested. The tradition of celebrating Plessy Day started in 2004, five years before Phoebe and Keith formed their foundation. That year, young people in New Orleans marked the day by leading a parade to Plessy Park from the nearby Frederick Douglass High School. The students had been studying New Orleans civil rights history and wrote stories about their personal connections to those events, as part of the Students at the Center writing program. The program published the student stories in an anthology called *The Long Ride*. After arriving at Plessy Park, the students performed skits on civil rights history.

The next year, 2005, the Crescent City Peace Alliance and other local groups persuaded the New Orleans City Council, the Louisiana Legislature, and the state's governor to declare that June 7th should be celebrated each year as an official day to honor the contributions that Homer Plessy and the Citizens' Committee made to Louisiana history. But two months after Plessy Day that year, Hurricane Katrina upended everything in New Orleans for quite a while, putting Plessy Day celebrations on hold for several years.

Since 2009, the year that Keith and Phoebe installed their first historical marker, the Plessy and Ferguson Foundation has hosted each year's Plessy Day events, often in partnership with the NOCCA Foundation. Their celebrations have included music, dance, and theater performances, as well as lectures and panel discussions on civil rights issues, and, one year, a Second Line parade. Jazz musician Carl LeBlanc composed a piece about Homer Plessy—"His Last Parade"—that LeBlanc's band has played at these events. "It's kind of our official tune," noted Keith.

The poster for the 2019 Plessy Day celebration, which occurred during the Plessy and Ferguson Foundation's 10th anniversary year.

PLESSY DAY

10th
ANNIVERSARY
JUNE 7
2019

EDUCATION
FOR
LIBERATION

Please join us as we honor the founders
of Straight University and celebrate 10
years of community programming and
marking New Orleans civil rights sites.

For more information:
504 921-3013
plessyandferguson.org
facebook.com/plessyandfergusonfoundation

Historic Marker Unveiling
Honoring Straight University and its Founders

Friday, June 7 at 6pm
Corner of Esplanade and N. Derbigny St.
Reception at Le Musée
de f.p.c. 6:30pm
2336 Esplanade Ave.

Special Guest Speaker
Judge Edwin Lombard

Music
Carl LeBlanc Trio
Troi Bechet

Light Refreshments
Free & Open to the Public

In Partnership with

Design by Noël Anderson

However, in June 2020, the Foundation decided not to hold a Plessy Day event. New Orleans and the rest of the nation were dealing with two major crises that June: the coronavirus pandemic and a new wave of civil rights protests. The pandemic was causing illness and death, hitting communities of color especially hard. Rules designed to slow the spread of the virus prohibited large public gatherings. Despite those rules, thousands had been joining large marches around the nation to protest recent killings of unarmed African Americans by police in Minneapolis, Louisville, and elsewhere. Instead of hosting a Plessy Day celebration that year, the Plessy and Ferguson Foundation released a video on its Facebook page on June 7, 2020, with the following text in stark black and white:

Plessy Day 2020
The Struggle Continues . . .
Today is Homer Plessy Day, the official day we have set aside to celebrate New Orleans' Black freedom fighters, educa-

tors, and entrepreneurs who have made this city great. But this Plessy Day is a day of mourning, not celebration. We mourn the loss of all who have died due to the Coronavirus pandemic. We mourn the fact that in the year 2020, our young people are still protesting in the streets against police brutality and for equal rights. On this day, we will remember the courage it took for Homer Plessy to sit in the whites only train car on June 7, 1892. And on this day, we stand with a new generation of freedom fighters until all systems of white supremacy are dismantled.

#DontBackDown #BlackLivesMatter

Mock Trials and More

Keith and Phoebe have also helped organize live re-enactments of the Homer Plessy court cases that bring together modern day judges and lawyers to play the parts of lawyers and judges from the 1890s. These "mock trials" help people understand the case's legal arguments. (The bibliography has a link to a re-enactment video.)

In addition, the Plessy and Ferguson Foundation has partnered with local groups to start a new organization, the New Orleans Arts and Culture Coalition. It holds exhibits and programs focusing on civil rights, human rights, and New Orleans history and culture. The coalition's first project was an exhibit on New Orleans African American history to mark the city's 300th birthday—its tricentennial—in 2018. The foundation hopes to work with other groups to create an African American History and Culture Trail, with a map available online to encourage visits to locations around New Orleans that played a part in the history of the city's people of color.

Current problems in New Orleans, from voting rights issues to education, also capture the attention of the Plessy and Ferguson Foundation. It has played a role in bringing attention to these situations. Phoebe continues making documentaries, including a series about conditions in local schools. Dr. Raynard Sanders, a member of the foundation's board, is also active in trying to improve the city's schools.

On another front, the foundation encouraged citizens to vote for an amendment to the Louisiana constitution that would repeal the 1898 rule that allowed people to be found guilty of felonies without all twelve jury members agreeing. The new amendment passed in November 2018. However, it applies only to new cases, not to those decided before 2018. Could earlier split-jury convictions be overturned? Yes, said the U.S. Supreme Court. In 2020, the court overturned the split-jury conviction of a Louisiana man who had appealed his conviction. The Supreme Court also said that from then on all states must require a unanimous jury vote for serious crimes. This ruling could help others convicted by split-jury votes in the past.

BURIED STORIES

"To have achieved what Smith W. Green did in New Orleans, with a building constructed for a Black man in 1908 to the highest architectural standards by the fanciest architecture firm in town at the height of Jim Crow when the rights and privileges of people of color were being rolled back is almost unbelievable to me, matched only by the fact that so many people have never heard about it," said Will Bradshaw, whose company brought Green's Pythian Temple back to life. "As a white Southerner, my forbears not only limited opportunity for African Americans, but we buried their stories. We didn't allow generations of African Americans to learn about what Mr. Green was able to achieve. We even buried the building, covering it in a horrible-looking metal façade for sixty years. The story of that building is emblematic of what I found interesting about becoming involved with Phoebe and Keith and their foundation. I was excited to collaborate with them because of the inspiration that comes from linking their two families, repairing the personal relationships that created segregation. We're going to tell those stories now. We're going to tell them in a new way."

© The NOCCA Institute, Elizabeth McMillan photo, New Orleans Center for Creative Arts Drama Department production of Se-Pa-Rate

In 2010, on the Plessy and Ferguson Foundation's second Plessy Day celebration, these New Orleans high school students performed the play Se-Pa-Rate, *which they created during after-school workshops at the NOCCA arts conservatory. In their play, the students explore the connection between their lives and the segregation that Homer Plessy confronted. Dasia Bell, the young woman marching forward, portrays the feeling that she doesn't truly belong to either of the two groups that are playing tug of war for her attention: people of color on one side and white people on the other.*

11

INSPIRING OTHERS

At the Plessy Day celebration in New Orleans in 2010, an interracial group of high school students performed *Se-Pa-Rate*, a play that they created themselves. It dealt with Homer Plessy's story as well as with examples of the many kinds of segregation that these teenagers experienced in their own lives. During six weeks of after-school workshops held at NOCCA, students from NOCCA and other local schools worked together to develop scenes for the play. According to the NOCCA Institute's website, in those workshops students explored the ways "they segregated themselves" by race, sexual orientation, and religion, as well as by "what music they liked, by which parent lived better after a divorce, whether they were in the main program at NOCCA or afterschool."

Silas Cooper, the school's drama teacher, oversaw this project and noted that at first some students were uncomfortable talking about these issues. "It was obvious that there were some cliques among the students," he explained. To encourage more interaction among the students, he kept changing the composition of the small groups that worked together. "Each time, students had to get in with another small group," he said. "The more they started to hear one another talk, things started to loosen up." One student said that writing the play "fostered acceptance and understanding that all of our stories count." Another noted, "The process made me

---

11

INSPIRING OTHERS

At the Plessy Day celebration in New Orleans in 2010, an interracial group of high school students performed *Se-Pa-Rate*, a play that they created themselves. It dealt with Homer Plessy's story as well as with examples of the many kinds of segregation that these teenagers experienced in their own lives. During six weeks of after-school workshops held at NOCCA, students from NOCCA and other local schools worked together to develop scenes for the play. According to the NOCCA Institute's website, in those workshops students explored the ways "they segregated themselves" by race, sexual orientation, and religion, as well as by "what music they liked, by which parent lived better after a divorce, whether they were in the main program at NOCCA or afterschool."

Silas Cooper, the school's drama teacher, oversaw this project and noted that at first some students were uncomfortable talking about these issues. "It was obvious that there were some cliques among the students," he explained. To encourage more interaction among the students, he kept changing the composition of the small groups that worked together. "Each time, students had to get in with another small group," he said. "The more they started to hear one another talk, things started to loosen up." One student said that writing the play "fostered acceptance and understanding that all of our stories count." Another noted, "The process made me

137

look at people a lot differently. I would defend them now, not laugh at someone" who seems "different." Another said that even at prom that year, "friends were discussing it." (See the opening of Chapter 2 for another photo from *Se-Pa-Rate*.)

Reaching Others

"Keith Plessy and Phoebe Ferguson have been trailblazers in making markers on African American history happen in New Orleans and in empowering other groups. They were an inspiration to us," said Dr. Erin Greenwald of the Louisiana Endowment for the Humanities. Spurred on by Keith and Phoebe's example, in 2018 Dr. Greenwald led a group supported by the New Orleans Tricentennial Commission that installed historical plaques on five buildings in New Orleans where there had once been slave markets. Before the end of the Civil War, more than 130,000 people of color were bought and sold at those markets and at others in New Orleans. Along with the plaques, there is also a New Orleans Slave Trade App. It lets people go online to learn more about the markets and hear readings from interviews with people who had been enslaved in Louisiana.

In 2018, Mark Roudané installed a historical marker of his own to celebrate the *L'Union* and *Tribune* newspapers, which led the fight for equal rights in New Orleans after the Civil War. Roudané is the great-great grandson of Dr. Louis Charles Roudanez, one of the founders of those activist newspapers. The new sign marks the entrance to the building where the newspapers had their offices.

The Plessy and Ferguson Foundation's historical markers have also inspired passers-by to do their own online research to learn more about the events that the markers describe. "It was a huge eye-opener," said Dr. Megan Holt, referring to the Homer Plessy marker she came across in 2010 when out for a walk with her fiancé near NOCCA. She grew up in Alabama and had been in New Orleans for seven years by then, working on her masters and doctorate degrees at Tulane University. "We were like: Wow, that happened here? Just four miles from where I was living!" She was surprised to learn details of the case from the marker's text that hadn't been taught at her public high school—"that it was a planned, deliberate action, that there was a Citizens' Committee, that it was a huge thing. The marker prompted me to learn more about the case. I'm glad it did." She is now the director of One Book One New Orleans, which promotes reading. Her new-found knowledge of Homer Plessy's story prompted her to persuade the authors of the book *Unfathomable City* to publish a new edition with a map of Plessy-related sites in the city. *Unfathomable City*, by Rebecca Solnit and Rebecca Snedeker, features illustrated maps that highlight key tourist sites in New Orleans. The book's authors and their publisher have been collaborating with the Plessy and Ferguson Foundation to identify places connected to the *Plessy v. Ferguson* story to put on the new edition's map.

"Folks are drawn to the Plessy and Ferguson Foundation because it exhibits poetic justice," noted Dr. Raynard Sanders, a member of the foundation's board of directors and a former New Orleans high school principal. Seeing those two families work together "drew me to work with them. I have a passion for history and the significance of important places. When I understood what they were doing, I thought it could have a lasting impact on generations to come. We are trying to unveil history. This history is not known by a lot of folks. When you bring to light these historical facts and the stories behind them, that has a way of changing people's perceptions. It doesn't happen overnight, but I think it will have an impact on the younger generation."

Listening to the Ghosts

"The symbolism of these two families coming together is clear and it's powerful," explained Dr. Kate Kokontis. "They are reclaiming public space to help people learn about and remember this history of organized resistance." When she came to watch the unveiling of the foundation's first marker at Plessy Park in 2009, she was a graduate student and had just heard Keith Weldon Medley give a talk about the Plessy story at the New Orleans Public Library. Since then, she has become a teacher at NOCCA, in its Academic Studio, and is now the assistant chair of the school's humanities department.

She and her Academic Studio colleagues have placed the history of NOCCA's location—so near where Homer Plessy was arrested—at the center of the school's humanities curriculum, along with "the histories of the systems and struggles that make it important."

The Plessy Park historical marker has had a major impact on her students, especially the 11th graders. They make a formal visit to the Plessy Park marker each spring after spending months taking a wide-ranging humanities course about the 18th and 19th centuries that explores "the rise of slavery, capitalism, and colonialism in the Atlantic world, and the resistance to those structures," explained Dr. Kokontis. "The course focuses on the causes of the Civil War, the possibilities of Reconstruction, the state-sanctioned terrorism and neglect that ended it, the efforts of the Citizens' Committee, and the heartbreak of the *Plessy v. Ferguson* decision." By the end of the course, students know the facts and "have the context to appreciate what happened on this site and why it's important."

At their Plessy Park ceremony each spring, she has students "read the marker out loud, and read the names of all the people on the Citizens' Committee, and talk about the ethical heart of the course." This course, which she and Dr. Jean-Marc Duplantier developed, is titled "Freedom and Haunting in Global Capitalist Modernity." It encourages the students to

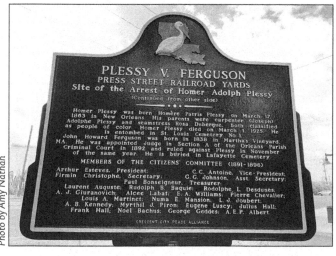

The Plessy Park historical marker's listing of the Citizens' Committee members.

Photo by Amy Nathan

"listen to the ghosts who are inhabiting the world around us, the hidden voices from past centuries, including ones we're encouraged not to hear, the ghosts that continue to speak to us and make claims on us in the present."

Dr. Kokontis feels that the work of the Citizens' Committee has a special message for students today. "It was an extensive and collaborative endeavor that had roots in lots of previous Black resistance and some interracial solidarity during Reconstruction and before. It's important to think not only about our obligations to the dead but also our obligations to the living and to each other, to look to this history of solidarity and collaboration. It shows that we don't have to be each other's enemies, unless we choose to be."

Beyond New Orleans

The Plessy and Ferguson Foundation's influence has spread beyond New Orleans. In 2020, a nationwide PBS TV special on the U.S. Constitution—*A More or Less Perfect Union*—featured interviews with Keith and Phoebe in which they discuss their goals for starting their foundation. In addition, Phoebe, Keith, and Keith's wife, Marietta Plessy, have traveled to other cities, often with author Keith Weldon Medley, to give talks encouraging others to do as they did—overcome historical and racial differences to come together. In 2009, they spoke at Central High School in Little Rock, Arkansas, at a ceremony marking the 52nd anniversary of one of the most dramatic confrontations in the effort to end segregated schools, when U.S. Army troops protected nine Black students as they integrated that school in 1957 (the year Phoebe and Keith were born). "To be invited to that place and meet some of the Little Rock Nine [as the nine students are called] was very special," recalled Keith Plessy.

So was receiving a standing ovation in 2010 when they spoke at a program on "Remembrance and Reconciliation" at Monroe Elementary School in Topeka, Kansas—one of the cities where the *Brown v. Board of Education* case started. The school building is now the site of the National Park Service's *Brown v. Board of Education* National Historic Site. In 1950, it was an all-Black elementary school that Linda Brown had to attend when she was turned away from a nearby white school in Topeka. This led her father, Oliver Brown, to file a complaint against the Topeka Board of Education. Twelve other Topeka parents joined the lawsuit because their children had also been turned away by a white school. The lawsuit became part of the famous case that the U.S. Supreme Court decided in 1954. Also part of the case were complaints against segregated schools in Delaware, South Carolina, Virginia, and Washington, D.C. The five complaints were combined into one case. Because Oliver Brown's name appeared first in the list of cases, the decision is called *Brown v. Board of Education*.

"We met Cheryl Brown Henderson that day, the sister of Linda Brown, and other members of the Brown family," said Keith Plessy. He and Phoebe have met others who are related to famous figures in civil rights history—both Black and white—including Lynne M. Jackson, a great-great-granddaughter of Dred Scott. In 2019, Keith and Phoebe participated in a Reconciliation Conference organized by the Dred

Descendants of other historic figures connected with civil rights that Keith and Phoebe have met with. From left to right: *Shannon LaNier, a descendant of President Thomas Jefferson; Lynne M. Jackson, great-great-granddaughter of Dred Scott; Bertram Hayes-Davis, great-great-great-grandson of Jefferson Davis, the president of the Confederacy; Cheryl Brown Henderson, sister of Linda Brown of the* Brown v. Board of Education *Supreme Court case.*

Courtesy Phoebe Ferguson

Scott Heritage Foundation. A panel discussion during the conference featured descendants of individuals involved in landmark civil rights cases. They discussed their thoughts about those cases and their feelings about the future. They are making plans to join with other descendants of civil rights figures to bring out a book that, as Keith explained, "would show how to get along with each other regardless of background, race, color, or creed."

Making it Personal

In 1997, Keith Plessy met another civil rights hero, Rosa Parks. Keith was just beginning to learn more about Homer Plessy, long before he met Phoebe Ferguson. He was working at a big New Orleans hotel where he often met the hotel's famous guests.

When Keith went to speak with Rosa Parks, she was sitting in a chair. "I kind of went down on one knee, kissed her hand, and said, 'Thank you for all your work,'" he recalled.

"Get up, boy," Rosa Parks said to Keith. "Your name is Plessy. You have work to do."

"I had no idea then what she meant, but I think I get it now," Keith explained. "I think what I'm doing now with the Plessy and Ferguson Foundation, I think that's what she meant. Whatever I learn, I want to pass it on to the next generation so it can benefit them."

Rosa Parks died in 2005, four years before the Plessy and Ferguson Foundation began. She didn't live to see that Keith took her advice.

Phoebe Ferguson also feels a responsibility to pass along important lessons she has learned. She recalled that when the foundation was getting started, some people said to her, "You didn't do this—rule against Homer Plessy. It was your relative who did that. Why are you feeling responsible for that?" She noted that such comments provided "an opportunity to begin a discussion on why it's important for white people to acknowledge this history—and take responsibility for learning it—that there was a time when white people's actions and beliefs hurt people of color, and how this history influenced the economic and social well-being of African Americans today." She added that, "You can't really have a dialogue on race unless we both have an understanding of what has occurred over the past 400 years. If you don't understand redlining, voter suppression, unequal pay, unequal education, and unequal access to jobs, then we're not on the same page with African Americans today. As Michael Eric Dyson wrote in his powerful book, *Tears We Cannot Stop*, 'When it comes to race, the past is always present.'"

For Phoebe, learning this history has been painful. "When I think about lynching, I feel sick to my stomach," she explained. "There are times when I can't look at those pictures. I can't read about that. But then I think: If I were Black and that was my history, I would feel that history so connected to me. It would be like having Peter Pan's shadow stitched onto me. If they're walking around with that pain that they can't help but carry with them, and if we as white people aren't acknowledging that we had a role in causing that pain, then we're living in an alternate universe. I care about history. Luckily, there are so many opportunities now to learn that history, with new museums opening that teach about slavery and lynching."

"It's a small form of reparations," noted Phoebe's daughter, Noël Anderson, describing the work of the foundation. She is a motion designer who also does a lot of graphic design.

"THE FRUIT OF YOUR LABORS"

For many years, few people remembered what Homer Plessy and the Citizens' Committee had done or the courage it took for them to stand up for racial justice in 1890s New Orleans. Louis Martinet, the editor of *The Crusader* newspaper and a leader of the Citizens' Committee, realized that their efforts might not succeed, nor win them praise at the time. In a letter to Albion Tourgée in 1893, Martinet wrote an epitaph that could serve for all of those who helped with their campaign: "You may not live to see the fruit of your labors and sacrifice, or to receive the gratitude of those benefited by them. It will be reserved to future generations to properly and justly estimate them." The Plessy and Ferguson Foundation is making sure that future generations remember.

The drawing that a 5th grader sent to Keith and Phoebe after they visited his school in 2012.

Courtesy Seth Osborne

Shortly after Katrina, she moved to New Orleans where she teaches at Loyola University of New Orleans. She handles all the graphics for the Plessy and Ferguson Foundation's posters and website. "Being from a wealthy family that lived for a long time in the South, there are implications with that. So I'm thrilled that my mom is putting in the work to change some of that legacy. It's work that needs to be done. The historic places need to be recognized, to maintain historical perspective about what the Black community in the city was and is. I have roots in New Orleans. I love the city."

The Plessy and Ferguson Foundation's historical markers help teach that history. Keith and Phoebe try to spread that history by speaking with school groups, from elementary schools to law schools. After one visit to a fifth-grade classroom, they received letters from the youngsters. "One of the letters has a drawing at the bottom of the page of someone with a face that's half white and half Black—which is supposed to be Keith and me," said Phoebe.

"That symbolism is hugely powerful. If we didn't do anything else than come together, we would still have a positive effect. But the foundation allows us to do so much more, to keep the legacy of this history alive and the importance of fighting for your rights if you're not really living the life that the constitution has promised us. What's amazing is to drive by a marker and watch people standing there reading the history of what happened on that spot, learning these amazing facts about what people did."

The Plessy v. Ferguson *historical marker in Plessy Park, with Ayo Scott's mural visible in the background, on the right in the photo.*

Courtesy Ayo Scott, photo by Amy Nathan

Courtesy Ayo Scott, photo by Amy Nathan

The photo above shows the full Ayo Scott mural in Plessy Park. His artwork spans more than half the length of a football field. The photo below shows one section of the mural, starting from where the arrow marker is located in the photo above and continuing to the mural's end, not far from where the park's historical marker stands.

Courtesy Ayo Scott, photo by Amy Nathan

AFTERWORD
Others Coming Together

O ther groups in the U.S. are also bridging differences that had placed them on opposite sides of racial issues in the past. They are working together on issues of reconciliation, social justice, and education, as the Plessy and Ferguson Foundation is doing. Sean Martin, a Baltimore high school history teacher who teaches about civil rights, noted that the Plessy and Ferguson Foundation and the other groups described here who are coming together show "that history isn't dead . . . that we too can be participants, playing important parts, big and small" in understanding that history and in not letting the past control how we think and feel today. Here are descriptions of other groups that are reaching across historical divides, as Keith Plessy and Phoebe Ferguson have been doing:

- *The Dred Scott Heritage Foundation*, created by descendants of Dred Scott—Lynne M. Jackson and her parents, John and Marsulite Madison—has worked with descendants of Roger B. Taney, the Supreme Court Chief Justice who authored the 1857 Dred Scott decision that kept Dred Scott enslaved and stated that African Americans could never be citizens. Members of these two families have worked to keep alive the story of Dred Scott and explain the great injustice that was done by that court decision. In addition, the Dred Scott Heritage Foundation has presented programs to discuss reconciliation. One such event was the Dred Scott Reconciliation Conference 2019 in St. Louis. It featured a panel with descendants linked to three pivotal civil rights court decisions. They discussed the cases and their influence today. Among the panelists were Lynne Jackson, Keith Plessy, Phoebe Ferguson, and Cheryl Brown Henderson.

Website: https://dredscottlives.org

- *Descendants of both President Thomas Jefferson and of Sally Hemings*, the enslaved woman who bore his children, have come together to teach about the pain and lasting impact that slavery has had on their families and the nation. Exhibits at Jefferson's Virginia home, Monticello, help people think about the effect of slavery.

    Website: https://www.monticello.org/site/about/thomas-jefferson-foundation

- *The Maryland Lynching Truth and Reconciliation Commission*, created in 2019 by a unanimous vote of the Maryland legislature, is the first state-wide commission in the U.S. formed to help citizens investigate lynching. The Commission hopes to bring together people in Maryland to study the forty documented lynchings that occurred in the state between 1865 and 1933, when the last known lynching in Maryland took place. A descendant of the African American man killed in that last lynching has been working with another group, the Maryland Lynching Memorial Project. This organization is coordinating with citizen coalitions to erect memorials and historical markers to help people acknowledge that lynching occurred and to honor and dignify the lives of the victims. The law establishing the Maryland Lynching Truth and Reconciliation Commission states: "Restorative justice requires a full knowledge, understanding, and acceptance of the truth before there can be any meaningful reconciliation."

    Website: https://www.mdlynchingmemorial.org

- *A Group of African American citizens in the Roanoke Rapids area of North Carolina*, led by Dr. Charles McCollum,

Sr., formed a committee (sponsored by Eastern Carolina Christian College), in order to enter a 2019 contest sponsored by the Z. Smith Reynolds Foundation to install an outdoor art monument about a "North Carolina person or group, especially women and people of color, whose story . . . is not often told." More than eighty communities entered the contest. The Roanoke Rapids team won one of the awards which enabled them to install a monument in the city's Martin Luther King, Jr., Park to honor Sarah Keys Evans. In 1952, as an African American member of the U.S. Women's Army Corps, she had been arrested in Roanoke Rapids for not moving to the back of an interstate bus. She protested her arrest before the Interstate Commerce Commission (ICC) and in 1955 she won her case. As a result, the ICC issued rules to end segregation in interstate travel. Most of the country obeyed the new regulations, but many in the South didn't until after the Freedom Rides of 1961. The regulations issued in her ICC decision helped end segregation on all public transportation (as described in books by Barnes, Nathan, and Roundtree, listed in the bibliography). The monument's unveiling took place on August 1, 2020—exactly sixty-eight years after Sarah Keys Evans boarded the bus in New Jersey that led to her arrest in Roanoke Rapids. Local citizens and elected officials—Black and white—supported the efforts to create this monument that honors her courage and can help bridge racial divisions that still exist.

Websites: https://www.zsrinclusivepublicart.com/#/
eastern-carolina-christian-college/
https://sarahkevansproject.com

- *The Joel Lane Museum House, Raleigh, North Carolina* installed a plaque in its garden in 2020 to honor the enslaved community who lived and labored on the plantation owned by Joel Lane (1739–1795). The plaque lists the names of the forty-three enslaved individuals whom researchers—using Joel Lane's will, slave auction and sales records, and other contemporary documents—have identified as having lived on the Lane plantation from its 1769 creation until the last of the enslaved were sold at auction in 1800, five years after Lane's death. Museum staff worked with members of the Raleigh African American community to create the plaque. At a dedication ceremony in February 2020, likely descendants of some of those named on the plaque unveiled the new memorial, and joined with a gathering of North Carolinians—white and Black— in reading aloud, in unison, the names of all forty-three individuals.

Website: https://www.joellane.org

- *The Equal Justice Initiative's Legacy Museum and National Memorial for Peace and Justice* in Montgomery, Alabama, encourage people to reflect on the impact that lynching and racial discrimination have had on the nation. People from around the country have worked together to collect soil samples from lynching sites that then become part of the museum's display and collection. The museum has documented thousands of lynchings that occurred throughout the nation after the Civil War.

Website: https://museumandmemorial.eji.org

The Resources section lists other museums and groups around the country that help people reflect on the nation's history of racial inequality.

TIME LINE

1682   French explorer La Salle gives Louisiana its name and claims it for France.

1718   French settlers establish the city of New Orleans.

1719   The first slave ship arrives in Louisiana with captives from Africa.

1769   Spain takes charge in Louisiana.

1803   France regains control of Louisiana and sells the territory that includes Louisiana to the United States.

1808   The U.S. stops participating in the international slave trade.

1811   Largest slave uprising in U.S. history occurs in Louisiana.

1812   Louisiana becomes a U.S. state.

1857   Dred Scott Supreme Court decision.

1861   Civil War begins as Louisiana and other southern states secede and form a new country, the Confederacy.

1862   U.S. Union Army troops defeat Confederate forces in New Orleans; *L'Union* newspaper is founded.

1863   The Emancipation Proclamation ends slavery in parts of the Confederacy that have not been defeated; Homer Plessy is born on March 17, 1863.*

1864   A new Louisiana state constitution ends slavery in Louisiana; *New Orleans Tribune* is founded.

1865   Civil War ends, the Confederacy is defeated; 13th Amendment ending slavery is added to the U.S. Constitution.

1866   Delegates trying to re-open Louisiana's Constitutional Convention to grant Black men the right to vote are attacked by a white mob.

1867   Protests end streetcar segregation in New Orleans.

1868   New Louisiana constitution gives Black men the right to vote, and officially ends school segregation; 14th Amendment is added to the U.S. Constitution establishing "equal protection" for all citizens; white mobs kill about 200 Black people in Opelousas in St. Landry Parish.

1870   15th Amendment is added to the U.S. Constitution giving Black men the right to vote; Louisiana legislature allows interracial marriage.

1873   As many as 150 people of color are killed trying to prevent an armed white group from taking over the Colfax courthouse.

1874   The White League militia tries to oust Louisiana's Republican governor and replace him with a Democrat; White League attacks New Orleans' integrated schools, forcing Black students to flee.

1877   U.S. Army troops are withdrawn from southern states; New Orleans schools are segregated again.

* Homer Plessy's tomb in New Orleans St. Louis Cemetery No. 1 says he was born in 1862. But an official copy of his birth certificate that author Keith Weldon Medley found during the research for his book, *We as Freemen*, shows that Plessy was born on St. Patrick's Day, March 17, 1863. Heather Green, a researcher for the Historic New Orleans Collection, found a 1900 census record that lists Plessy's birth as "March 1863."

1889   *The Crusader* newspaper is founded.

1890   Louisiana legislature passes the Separate Car Act.

1891   Comité des Citoyens (Citizens' Committee) is founded to overturn the Separate Car Act.

1892   Homer Plessy is arrested on June 7th for sitting in a train car for white passengers; Judge John Howard Ferguson finds Homer Plessy guilty of breaking the Separate Car Act.

1894   Louisiana law makes interracial marriage illegal again.

1896   *Plessy v. Ferguson* Supreme Court decision.

1898   New Louisiana constitution makes it hard for Black men to vote, requires separate schools for Black and white students, and allows non-unanimous jury votes for felony convictions.

1902   Streetcars in New Orleans are segregated again.

1909   NAACP is founded.

1920   19th Amendment added to the U.S. Constitution giving women the right to vote.

1925   Homer Plessy dies on March 1, 1925.

1928   Segregation is extended to Louisiana buses and other public transit vehicles.

1942   A. P. Tureaud, Sr., wins a lawsuit to give African American teachers in New Orleans the right to have equal pay with white teachers.

1950   Black students gain the right to attend law school at Louisiana State University.

1953   A. P. Tureaud, Jr., is the first Black student to register as an undergraduate at Louisiana State University, but his right to register is soon rescinded.

1954   *Brown v. Board of Education* Supreme Court decision.

1955   Rosa Parks refuses to move to the back of a bus in Montgomery, Alabama.

1957   Keith Plessy and Phoebe Ferguson are born.

1958   A. P. Tureaud, Sr. lawsuit ends streetcar and bus segregation in New Orleans.

1960   New Orleans begins to end segregation in its public schools; sit-ins and boycotts in New Orleans protest businesses that discriminate against people of color.

1961   Freedom Rides protests.

1964   U.S. Civil Rights Act; 24th Amendment ends poll taxes; first group of Black students successfully register as undergraduates at Louisiana State University.

1965   U.S. Voting Rights Act.

1967   Keith Plessy learns in school that he might be related to Homer Plessy; U.S. Supreme Court allows interracial marriage.

1968   U.S. Fair Housing Act.

1979   Keith Plessy paints portraits of Black heroes in Valena C. Jones Elementary School.

1996   Keith Plessy meets Keith Weldon Medley, author of *We as Freemen*, and learns that Homer Plessy was his great-grandfather's cousin; Keith Plessy and family attend 100th anniversary commemoration of the *Plessy v. Ferguson* decision.

1997   Keith Plessy meets Rosa Parks.

2002   Phoebe Ferguson learns that Judge John Howard Ferguson was her great-great-grandfather.

2004   Keith Plessy meets Phoebe Ferguson.

2005   June 7th is officially declared to be observed as Plessy Day in Louisiana; Hurricane Katrina causes great damage in New Orleans.

2009   Plessy and Ferguson Foundation is started; its first historical marker is installed.

2018   The street where Homer Plessy was arrested is renamed Homer Plessy Way; Louisiana voters pass an amendment to their constitution requiring unanimous jury verdicts for felony convictions, overturning the split-jury rule from the 1898 constitution.

ABOUT THE PLESSY AND FERGUSON FOUNDATION

Mission Statement for the Plessy and Ferguson Foundation (www.PlessyandFerguson.org): "The primary mission of the Plessy and Ferguson Foundation is to teach the history of the *Plessy v. Ferguson* case and why it is still relevant today." The foundation, a 501(c)3 non-profit organization, engages in education, preservation, and outreach efforts that are described on its website. In 2017 the foundation received an award from Preserve Louisiana, honoring the foundation's role in preserving Louisiana's civil rights history. (Half of the royalties earned on the sale of this book will be donated to the Plessy and Ferguson Foundation.)

FAMILY TREES

The Ferguson Family Tree on the next page shows only the direct Ferguson family line from Judge John Howard Ferguson to Phoebe Ferguson. It doesn't include all the siblings in each generation and doesn't go back to the first of her Ferguson relatives to come to North America. They left Scotland in the 1650s and settled in Massachusetts.

The Plessy Family Tree (on the following two pages) shows only the direct Plessy family line to Homer Plessy and to Keith Plessy. It doesn't include additional siblings in each generation. The first couple on this tree are commonly known today as Agnes Mathieu and Mathieu Devaux, but the tree shows their full names. They had seven children who all used the last name Mathieu (as noted in Chapter 8). The tree in this book shows only one of their children, Catherina/Catiche, because she is the one who leads directly to both Homer Plessy as well as to Keith Plessy.

Homer Plessy's tomb in New Orleans lists his birth year as 1862, but author Keith Weldon Medley found Homer Plessy's original birth certificate; it shows that Homer Plessy's birthdate was March 17, 1863, St. Patrick's Day. His name on his birth certificate is listed as: Homere Patris Plessy. However, later in life, he came to be known as Homer Adolph Plessy, the name used when his case was argued at the Louisiana Supreme Court and the name listed on his tomb. In 1892, when he signed an official court document, he wrote, "H. A. Plessy."

Keith Plessy, Phoebe Ferguson, Bobby Duplissey, and Michael Nolden Henderson provided the names and dates for these family trees. Phoebe Ferguson's daughter, Noël Anderson, created the design for the trees. Noël is a graphic artist and motion designer based in New Orleans who teaches at Loyola University of New Orleans; she does all the graphic design for the Plessy and Ferguson Foundation.

FERGUSON
FAMILY TREE

 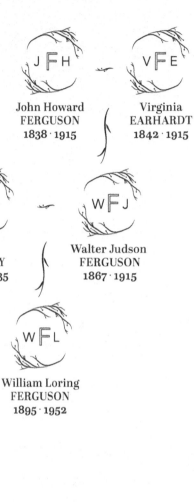

John Howard
FERGUSON
1838 · 1915

Virginia
EARHARDT
1842 · 1915

Indie
GIFFNEY
1870 · 1935

Walter Judson
FERGUSON
1867 · 1915

Rebecca
BOWEN
1895 · 1984

William Loring
FERGUSON
1895 · 1952

Anne
WILLIAMS
1931 · 1990

William Loring
FERGUSON, JR.
1925 · 1967

Phoebe Chase
FERGUSON
1957

KEY:

 Married

Parents of

PLESSY
FAMILY TREE

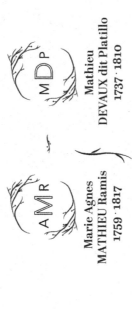

Mathieu
DEVAUX dit Platillo
1737 · 1810

Marie Agnes
MATHIEU Ramis
1759 · 1817

Catherina/Catiche
MATHIEU
1782 · 1848

Francois Germain
PLESSY
1777 · 1863

Clara
MATHIEU
1827 · 1899

Honore Joseph Gustave
PLESSY
1806 · 1892

Joseph Adolphe
PLESSY
1822 · 1869

Rosalie
DEBERGUE
1835 · 1913

P P J
Philomene
JOSEPH
1859 · 1944

S P W
Sedonia
WHITE
1889 · 1970

M P B
Marie Verna Mae
BLANCHARD
1926 · 1976

J P G
Joseph Gustave
PLESSY
1850 · 1924

G P J
Gustave Joseph
PLESSY
1885 · 1957

P P G
Paul Gustave
PLESSY
1929 · 2014

K P M
Keith M.
PLESSY
1957

V P B
Virginia Louise
BOURDENAVE
1868 · 1949

H P A
Homer Patris Adolph
PLESSY
1863 · 1925

KEY:

⟶ Married

⎰ Parents of

HISTORICAL MARKER
HOW-TO GUIDE

Each state has its own rules for how to have a historical marker installed. Here are the rules that the Plessy and Ferguson Foundation has to follow in Louisiana.

- A marker can't honor a living person. The person must have done something worth honoring that occurred at least fifty years ago.
- An event must have taken place at least fifty years ago to be honored, but there can be exceptions if a more recent event is especially important.
- "We had to do research and work with historians to write the text for a marker," explained Phoebe. Only a certain number of lines of text fit on the size of historical marker that the state uses.
- They also had to choose a good location for the marker— near a place connected to the event or the person to be honored—a spot where people passing by can read the marker and where it's safe to stand to view it. Placing it on public land is best because otherwise you need permission from the person who owns the land, as happened with the Homer Plessy marker on the land owned by the NOCCA Foundation.

Courtesy Phoebe Ferguson

Installing and unveiling the McDonogh 19 Elementary School historical marker.

- After writing the text, they had to fill out an application and submit it to the Louisiana Office of Tourism to make sure it met the basic rules. They also had to submit photocopies of information from at least three books or other sources to support the facts in the text. Then the application, text, and supporting materials went to the Department of History at Louisiana State University for historians to check for accuracy.
- After the historians gave their OK, the application and text went to the Louisiana Tourism Development Commission. It meets once a year in August to review all applications for historical markers and decide which ones to approve.
- After a marker is approved, the sponsoring group has to pay to have the marker made. In Louisiana, that costs from $2,000 to $2,500 depending on how many letters are in the text.
- "If it's on public property, the Department of Transportation installs it. If it's on private property, you have to figure out another way to have it installed," said Phoebe.

HISTORICAL MARKERS

The following photos show the text on both sides of the five historical markers the Plessy and Ferguson Foundation had installed by the end of 2019.

Photo by Amy Nathan

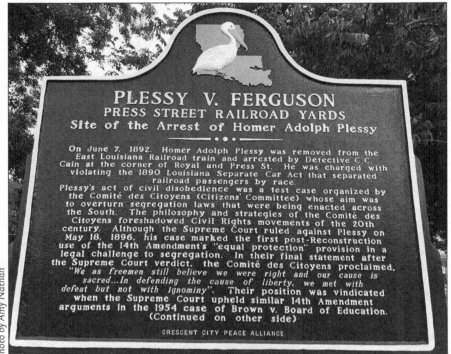

PLESSY V. FERGUSON
PRESS STREET RAILROAD YARDS
Site of the Arrest of Homer Adolph Plessy

On June 7, 1892, Homer Adolph Plessy was removed from the East Louisiana Railroad train and arrested by Detective C.C. Cain at the corner of Royal and Press St. He was charged with violating the 1890 Louisiana Separate Car Act that separated railroad passengers by race.

Plessy's act of civil disobedience was a test case organized by the Comité des Citoyens (Citizens' Committee) whose aim was to overturn segregation laws that were being enacted across the South. The philosophy and strategies of the Comité des Citoyens foreshadowed Civil Rights movements of the 20th century. Although the Supreme Court ruled against Plessy on May 18, 1896, his case marked the first post-Reconstruction use of the 14th Amendment's "equal protection" provision in a legal challenge to segregation. In their final statement after the Supreme Court verdict, the Comité des Citoyens proclaimed, "We as freemen still believe we were right and our cause is sacred...In defending the cause of liberty, we met with defeat but not with ignominy". Their position was vindicated when the Supreme Court upheld similar 14th Amendment arguments in the 1954 case of Brown v. Board of Education. (Continued on other side)

CRESCENT CITY PEACE ALLIANCE

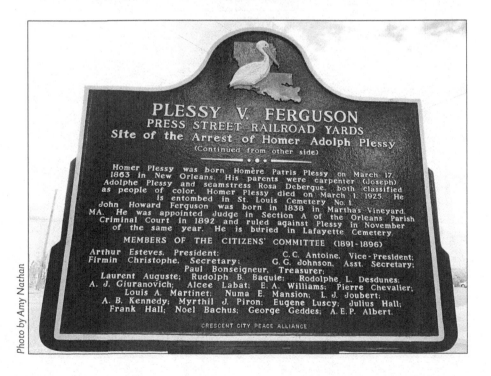

Photo by Amy Nathan

PLESSY V. FERGUSON
PRESS STREET RAILROAD YARDS
Site of the Arrest of Homer Adolph Plessy
(Continued from other side)

Homer Plessy was born Homère Patris Plessy on March 17, 1863 in New Orleans. His parents were carpenter (Joseph) Adolphe Plessy and seamstress Rosa Debergue, both classified as people of color. Homer Plessy died on March 1, 1925. He is entombed in St. Louis Cemetery No. 1.

John Howard Ferguson was born in 1838 in Martha's Vineyard, MA. He was appointed Judge in Section A of the Orleans Parish Criminal Court in 1892 and ruled against Plessy in November of the same year. He is buried in Lafayette Cemetery.

MEMBERS OF THE CITIZENS' COMMITTEE (1891-1896)

Arthur Esteves, President; C.C. Antoine, Vice-President; Firmin Christophe, Secretary; G.G. Johnson, Asst. Secretary; Paul Bonseigneur, Treasurer; Laurent Auguste; Rudolph B. Baquie; Rodolphe L. Desdunes; A. J. Giuranovich; Alcee Labat; E. A. Williams; Pierre Chevalier; Louis A. Martinet; Numa E. Mansion; L. J. Joubert; A. B. Kennedy; Myrthil J. Piron; Eugene Luscy; Julius Hall; Frank Hall; Noel Bachus; George Geddes; A.E.P. Albert.

CRESCENT CITY PEACE ALLIANCE

HISTORICAL MARKERS

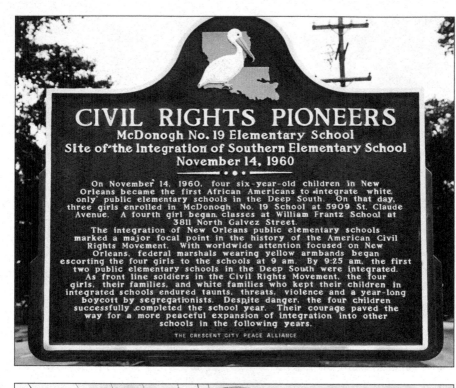

CIVIL RIGHTS PIONEERS
McDonogh No. 19 Elementary School
Site of the Integration of Southern Elementary School
November 14, 1960

On November 14, 1960, four six-year-old children in New Orleans became the first African Americans to integrate white, only public elementary schools in the Deep South. On that day, three girls enrolled in McDonogh No. 19 School at 5909 St. Claude Avenue. A fourth girl began classes at William Frantz School at 3811 North Galvez Street.

The integration of New Orleans public elementary schools marked a major focal point in the history of the American Civil Rights Movement. With worldwide attention focused on New Orleans, federal marshals wearing yellow armbands began escorting the four girls to the schools at 9 am. By 9:25 am, the first two public elementary schools in the Deep South were integrated.

As front line soldiers in the Civil Rights Movement, the four girls, their families, and white families who kept their children in integrated schools endured taunts, threats, violence and a year-long boycott by segregationists. Despite danger, the four children successfully completed the school year. Their courage paved the way for a more peaceful expansion of integration into other schools in the following years.

THE CRESCENT CITY PEACE ALLIANCE

Courtesy Phoebe Ferguson

HISTORY

The integration of New Orleans schools was part of a larger action by the NAACP to end segregated schools nationwide. Since the Plessy v. Ferguson decision in 1896, schools across the Deep South were rigidly segregated based on race. Although they were supposed to be equal in quality to white schools, the black schools received subpar facilities and educational materials.

In September 1952 with assistance from attorneys Thurgood Marshall and Robert Carter of the NAACP Legal Defense and Educational Fund, New Orleans attorney A.P. Tureaud initiated a suit on behalf of Earl Benjamin Bush calling for an end to the segregated school system in Orleans parish. In 1954, the United States Supreme Court set aside the Plessy decision and ruled that segregated schools are unconstitutional. The high court ordered that public schools be desegregated "with all deliberate speed." In 1956, the US Court of Appeals dismissed multiple attempts by the Louisiana Legislature to thwart integration efforts.

In July 1959, Federal Judge J. Skelly Wright ordered the Orleans Parish School Board to integrate its schools. After a series of aptitude tests, the four girls were selected to integrate McDonogh 19 and William Frantz schools in the New Orleans Ninth Ward.

THE PLESSY & FERGUSON FOUNDATION

Courtesy Phoebe Ferguson

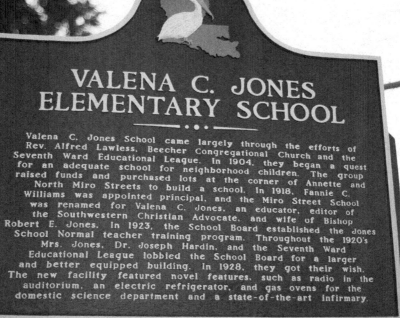

VALENA C. JONES ELEMENTARY SCHOOL

· • • ·

Valena C. Jones School came largely through the efforts of Rev. Alfred Lawless, Beecher Congregational Church and the Seventh Ward Educational League. In 1904, they began a quest for an adequate school for neighborhood children. The group raised funds and purchased lots at the corner of Annette and North Miro Streets to build a school. In 1918, Fannie C. Williams was appointed principal, and the Miro Street School was renamed for Valena C. Jones, an educator, editor of the Southwestern Christian Advocate, and wife of Bishop Robert E. Jones. In 1923, the School Board established the Jones School Normal teacher training program. Throughout the 1920's Mrs. Jones, Dr. Joseph Hardin, and the Seventh Ward Educational League lobbied the School Board for a larger and better equipped building. In 1928, they got their wish. The new facility featured novel features, such as radio in the auditorium, an electric refrigerator, and gas ovens for the domestic science department and a state-of-the-art infirmary.

Courtesy Phoebe Ferguson

FANNIE C. WILLIAMS
PIONEER IN PUBLIC EDUCATION

· • • ·

As one of New Orleans' premier educators in the first half of the twentieth century, Fannie C. Williams steered this school through decades of challenge and change. An active civic leader, she was nationally recognized and appointed to three presidential commissions. A tribute to her stature can be seen from the list of guests that appeared at the school during her tenure. They included first lady, Eleanor Roosevelt; Harlem Renaissance writer, James Weldon Johnson; renowned educator, Mary McLeod Bethune; Dr. W. E. B. Dubois; scientist, Dr. George Washington Carver; historian, Dr. Carter G. Woodson; track star, Jesse Owens; and writer and lecturer, Dale Carnegie visited the school as well as many others.

Courtesy Phoebe Ferguson

THE PYTHIAN TEMPLE

The architecturally acclaimed Pythian Temple building at 234 Loyola Avenue (formerly South Saratoga) is one of New Orleans' storied landmarks. From 1908 to 1941, members of the Knights of Pythias, under the leadership of Smith W. Green, served as a beacon of pride for African Americans during the segregation era of Jim Crow. In June of 1908, the Pythians laid their cornerstone at Gravier and Saratoga Streets. In August of 1909, Green opened the Pythian Temple at a cost of over $200,000. The dedication ceremonies featured orchestral music and selections by the St. James A. M. E. choir and glee club of the Dryades Street YMCA. Black lawyer, J. Madison Vance — a 1912 delegate to the Republican National Convention — engendered frequent applause as he spoke of the "Power of Organization and its effects upon Civilization." The Times-Picayune described the Pythian Temple as "the biggest business enterprise ever attempted by the colored race in the United States."

(Continued on other side)

SPONSORED BY THE PLESSY AND FERGUSON FOUNDATION

Courtesy Phoebe Ferguson

THE PYTHIAN TEMPLE

(Continued from other side)

• • •

Many of the masonic and social lodges held meetings in the Pythian Temple. The Temple's seven-story structure contained office suites, a combination theater and auditorium, and a rooftop garden for dancing. *Architectural Art and its Allies* recognized it in its March 1908 edition. Musicians Louis Armstrong, Manuel Manetta, and Manuel Perez entertained there.

SMITH W. GREEN

Smith W. Green became leader of the Grand Lodge, Colored Order of the Knights of Pythias of Louisiana. He was a former slave, who became wealthy as a grocer, and subsequently became president of the Liberty Independence Insurance company. He was also on the executive committee of the local NAACP in New Orleans and worked closely with famed New Orleans lawyer, A. P. Tureaud, as they lobbied for a new hospital for veterans. He was elected Supreme Chancellor of the Knights of Pythias of Louisiana in 1908. The Pythian Temple was Green's crowning achievement.

SPONSORED BY GCE, ERG ENTERPRISES, CCCLT INC,
STUDIOWTA, LANDIS CONSTRUCTION

Courtesy Phoebe Ferguson

STRAIGHT UNIVERSITY

In 1869, the American Missionary Association (AMA) and philanthropist Seymour Straight partnered to found Straight University, a school where African Americans could aspire to the highest education available after Emancipation. Classes were first held in a Congregational church, but by 1871, a main university building was erected on the northeast corner of Esplanade Avenue and N. Derbigny Street.

As Union soldiers left New Orleans in 1877, the main university building was set ablaze in an act of arson. The structure was completely demolished and the campus relocated to the corner of Canal Street and Tonti Street. In 1930, Straight merged with New Orleans University to form Dillard University, Louisiana's oldest historically black university.

(Continued on other side)

SPONSORED BY DILLARD UNIVERSITY AND
PRESERVATION RESOURCE CENTER OF NEW ORLEANS

Photo by Amy Nathan

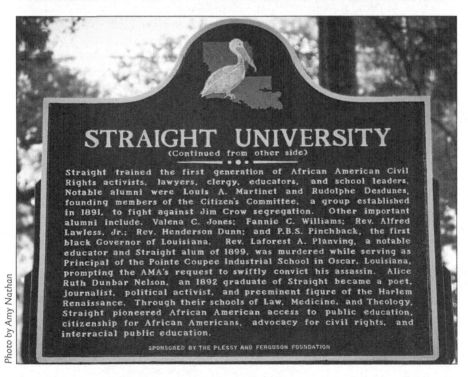

STRAIGHT UNIVERSITY
(Continued from other side)

Straight trained the first generation of African American Civil Rights activists, lawyers, clergy, educators, and school leaders. Notable alumni were Louis A. Martinet and Rudolphe Desdunes, founding members of the Citizen's Committee, a group established in 1891, to fight against Jim Crow segregation. Other important alumni include: Valena C. Jones; Fannie C. Williams; Rev. Alfred Lawless, Jr.; Rev. Henderson Dunn; and P.B.S. Pinchback, the first black Governor of Louisiana. Rev. Laforest A. Planving, a notable educator and Straight alum of 1899, was murdered while serving as Principal of the Pointe Coupee Industrial School in Oscar, Louisiana, prompting the AMA's request to swiftly convict his assassin. Alice Ruth Dunbar Nelson, an 1892 graduate of Straight became a poet, journalist, political activist, and preeminent figure of the Harlem Renaissance. Through their schools of Law, Medicine, and Theology, Straight pioneered African American access to public education, citizenship for African Americans, advocacy for civil rights, and interracial public education.

SPONSORED BY THE PLESSY AND FERGUSON FOUNDATION

Photo by Amy Nathan

HISTORICAL MARKERS

RESOURCES

Focused on New Orleans

Amistad Research Center—http://www.amistadresearchcenter.org
CreoleGen (on Creole history)—www.creolegen.org
Louis A. Martinet Society (Lawyer's organization in New Orleans
   that A. P. Tureaud, Sr., helped start in 1957, named in honor of
   the Citizens' Committee leader)—http://gnomartinet.com
Hidden History Tours—https://www.hiddenhistory.us
The Historic New Orleans Collection—https://www.hnoc.org
LA Creole: Louisiana Creole Research Association—https://
   lacreole.org
Le Musee de f.p.c. (Museum honoring New Orleans' Free People of
   Color)—https://www.lemuseedefpc.com
Louisiana Endowment for the Humanities—https://www.leh.org
Midlo Center for New Orleans Studies—https://scholarworks.uno.
   edu/midlo/
New Orleans African American Museum—https://www.noaam.org
The New Orleans Arts & Culture Coalition—https://www.
   artscultureco.org
One Book One New Orleans—http://onebookonenola.org
Paper Monuments (explores stories of New Orleans through art
   and storytelling)—https://www.papermonuments.org
Plessy and Ferguson Foundation—www.PlessyandFerguson.org
Preservation Resource Center of New Orleans—https://prcno.org
Roudanez Website—https://roudanez.com

Focused on Historic Civil Rights Cases and Other African American History

Brown Foundation—https://brownvboard.org
Dred Scott Heritage Foundation—https://dredscottlives.org
Equal Justice Initiative—https://museumandmemorial.eji.org
Joel Lane House Museum—https://www.joellane.org
Leona Tate Foundation for Change—www.LeonaTateFoundation.
  org
Little Rock Nine Foundation—https://littlerock9.com/index.html
Martin Luther King, Jr. Center for Nonviolent Social Change—
  http://www.thekingcenter.org/about-king-center
Maryland Lynching Memorial Project—https://www.
  mdlynchingmemorial.org
National Museum of African American History and Culture—
  https://nmaahc.si.edu
Reginald F. Lewis Museum of Maryland African American History
  and Culture—https://lewismuseum.org
Ruby Bridges Foundation—http://46679212.weebly.com/the-ruby-
  bridges-foundation.html
Thomas Jefferson Foundation—https://www.monticello.org/site/
  about/thomas-jefferson-foundation
Whitney Plantation—http://www.whitneyplantation.com

Texts of the Main Sections of Three Post-Civil War Amendments to U. S. Constitution

13th Amendment to the U.S. Constitution
Ratified 1865

> SECTION 1. Neither slavery nor involuntary servitude, except
> as a punishment for crime whereof the party shall have been
> duly convicted, shall exist within the United States, or any place
> subject to their jurisdiction.

14th Amendment to the U.S. Constitution
Ratified 1868

> SECTION 1. All persons born or naturalized in the United
> States, and subject to the jurisdiction thereof, are citizens of
> the United States and of the state wherein they reside. No state
> shall make or enforce any law which shall abridge the privileges
> or immunities of citizens of the United States; nor shall any
> state deprive any person of life, liberty, or property, without due
> process of law; nor deny to any person within its jurisdiction the
> equal protection of the laws.

15th Amendment to the U.S. Constitution
Ratified 1870

SECTION 1. The right of citizens of the United States to vote shall not be denied or abridged by the United States or by any state on account of race, color, or previous condition of servitude.

BIBLIOGRAPHY

Interviews with Author
(by phone except where noted)

Noël Anderson, October 15, 2019
Will Bradshaw, July 11, 2019
Dr. Mary Lane Cobb, March 8, 2020, in person, and via email
Silas Cooper, September 6, 2019
Bobby Duplissey, August 26, 2019
Phoebe Ferguson, February 20, 2018; March 17, 2018; August 21, 2019
Heather Green, August 8, 2019, via email
Dr. Erin Greenwald, October 2, 2018
Michael Nolden Henderson, September 6 and 9, 2019
Megan Holt, June 13, 2019
Lanie Hubbard, March 12, 2020
Lynne M. Jackson, September 30, 2019, via email
Dr. Kate Kokontis, July 14, 2019
Francis X. Norton, Jr., March 4, 2020, via email
Seth Osborne, September 22, 2019
Keith M. Plessy, February 28, 2018; July 3, 2018; August 21, 2019
Dr. Raynard Sanders, June 12, 2019
Will Schwartz, November 30, 2018
Ayo Scott, June 18, 19 and August 29, 2019, via email
Jerome Smith, March 18, 2011, in person, as part of an educational
    program at Martin Luther King, Jr., Charter School in New
    Orleans; that interview was donated in 2019 to the Oral History
    collection of the Historic New Orleans Collection.

Rev. Brenda B. Square, January 4, 2020, via email
Leona Tate, November 25, 2018
A. P. Tureaud, Jr., November 5, 2019, via email

Books

Arsenault, Raymond. *Freedom Riders: 1961 and the Struggle for Racial Justice*. New York: Oxford University Press, 2006.

Baker, Liva. *The Second Battle of New Orleans: The Hundred-Year Struggle to Integrate the Schools*. New York: Harper Collins, 1996.

Baldino, Thomas J., and Kyle L. Kreider. *Of the People, by the People, for the People: A Documentary Record of Voting Rights and Electoral Reform*. Westport, CT: Greenwood, 2010.

Barnes, Catherine A. *Journey from Jim Crow: The Desegregation of Southern Transit*. New York: Columbia University Press, 1983.

Bauer, Shane. *American Prison*. New York: Penguin Press, 2018.

Bell, Caryn Cossé. *Revolution, Romanticism, and the Afro-Creole Protest Tradition in Louisiana 1718–1868*. Baton Rouge: Louisiana State University Press, 1997.

Bridges, Ruby. *Through My Eyes*. New York: Scholastic, 1999.

Broom, Sarah. *The Yellow House*. New York: Grove Press, 2019.

Clark, Emily. *The Strange History of the American Quadroon: Free Women of Color in the Revolutionary Atlantic World*. Chapel Hill: University of North Carolina Press, 2013.

Coles, Robert. *The Story of Ruby Bridges*. New York: Scholastic Press, 1995.

DeSantis, John. *The Thibodaux Massacre: Racial Violence and the 1887 Sugar Cane Labor Strike*. Charleston, SC: The History Press, 2016.

Desdunes, Rodolphe Lucien. *Our People and Our History: Fifty Creole Portraits*. Baton Rouge: Louisiana State University Press, 1911, 1973.

DeVore, Donald E., and Joseph Logsdon. *Crescent City Schools: Public Education in New Orleans 1841–1991*. Lafayette: University of Louisiana at Lafayette Press, 1991.

Du Bois, W. E. B. *Black Reconstruction in America: 1860–1880*. New York: The Free Press, 1935.

Dyson, Michael Eric. *Tears We Cannot Stop: A Sermon to White America*. New York: St. Martin's Press, 2017.

Elliott, Mark. *Justice Deferred: Albion Tourgeé and the Fight for Civil Rights*. Chautauqua, NY: Chautauqua County Historical Society, 2008.

Foner, Eric. *Reconstruction: America's Unfinished Revolution, 1863–1877*. New York: Harper Perennial, 1988.

———. *The Second Founding: How the Civil War and Reconstruction Remade the Constitution*. New York: W. W. Norton, 2019.

Gates, Henry Louis, Jr. *Stony the Road: Reconstruction, White Suprem-acy, and the Rise of Jim Crow*. New York: Penguin Press, 2019.

Hall, Gwendolyn Midlo. *Africans in Colonial Louisiana: The Development of Afro-Creole Culture in the Eighteenth Century*. Baton Rouge: Louisiana State University Press, 1995.

Henderson, Michael Nolden. *Got Proof!: My Genealogical Journey Through the Use of Documentation*. Suwanee, GA: The Write Image, 2013.

Hollandsworth, James G., Jr. *An Absolute Massacre: The New Orleans Race Riot of July 30, 1866*. Baton Rouge: Louisiana State University Press, 2001.

Johnson, Walter. *Soul by Soul: Life Inside the Antebellum Slave Market*. Cambridge: Harvard University Press, 1999.

Kein, Sybil. *Creole: The History and Legacy of Louisiana's Free People of Color*. Baton Rouge: Louisiana State University Press, 2000.

Keith, LeeAnna. *The Colfax Massacre*. New York: Oxford University Press, 2008.

Kelley, Blair L. M. *Right to Ride: Streetcar Boycotts and African American Citizenship in the Era of Plessy v. Ferguson*. Chapel Hill, NC: University of North Carolina Press, 2010.

Lane, Charles. *The Day Freedom Died: The Colfax Massacre, the Supreme Court, and the Betrayal of Reconstruction*. New York: Henry Holt and Company, 2008.

LeDoux, Jerome G. *War of the Pews: A Personal Account of St. Augustine Church in New Orleans*. Donaldsonville, LA: Margaret Media, 2011.

Lepore, Jill. *These Truths: A History of the United States*. New York: W. W. Norton, 2018.

Lewinson, Paul. *Race, Class and Party: A History of Negro Suffrage and White Politics in the South*. New York: Oxford University Press, 1932.

Luxenberg, Steve. *Separate: The Story of Plessy v. Ferguson, and America's Journey from Slavery to Segregation*. New York: W. W. Norton, 2019.

Mancini, Matthew J. *One Dies, Get Another: Convict Leasing in the American South, 1866–1928*. Columbia, SC: University of South Carolina Press, 1996.

McWhorter, Diane. *A Dream of Freedom: The Civil Rights Movement from 1954 to 1968*. New York: Scholastic, 2004.

Medley, Keith Weldon. *Black Life in Old New Orleans*. Gretna, LA: Pelican Publishing Company, 2014.

——— *We as Freemen: Plessy v. Ferguson*. Gretna, LA: Pelican Publishing Company, 2003.

Murray, Pauli, ed. *States' Laws on Race and Color*. Athens, GA: The University of Georgia Press, 1997, paperback 2016.

Nathan, Amy. *Round and Round Together: Taking a Merry-go-Round Ride into the Civil Rights Movement*. Philadelphia: Paul Dry Books, 2011.

———. *Take a Seat—Make a Stand: A Hero in the Family, the Story of Sarah Keys Evans*. New York: iUniverse, 2006.

Nystrom, Justin A. *New Orleans after the Civil War: Race, Politics, and a New Birth of Freedom*. Baltimore: Johns Hopkins University Press, 2010.

Rasmussen, Daniel. *American Uprising: The Untold Story of America's Largest Slave Revolt*. New York: Harper Perennial, 2012.

Rice, T. D., and W. T. Lhamon, Jr. *Jim Crow, American: Selected Songs and Plays*. Cambridge: Harvard University Press, 2003, 2009.

Robinson, Plater. *A House Divided: A Teaching Guide on the History of Civil Rights in Louisiana*, 2nd Edition. Southern Institute for Education and Research, Tulane University, 1995.

Rogers, Kim Lacy. *Righteous Lives: Narratives of the New Orleans Civil Rights Movement*. New York: New York University Press, 1993.

Rothstein, Richard. *The Color of Law: A Forgotten History of How our Government Segregated America*. New York: W. W. Norton, 2017.

Roundtree, Dovey Johnson, and Katie McCabe. *Mighty Justice: My Life in Civil Rights*. Chapel Hill: Algonquin Books, 2019.

Sanders, Raynard, David Stovall, and Terrenda White. *Twenty-First Century Jim Crow Schools: The Impact of Charters on Public Education*. Boston: Beacon Press, 2018.

Schafer, Judith Kelleher. *Becoming Free, Remaining Free: Manumission and Enslavement in New Orleans, 1846–1862*. Baton Rouge: Louisiana State University Press, 2003.

Shaik, Fatima. *Melitte*. New York: Dial, 1997.

Southern, Eileen. *The Music of Black Americans: A History*. New York: W. W. Norton, 1997.

Spear, Jennifer M. *Race, Sex, and Social Order in Early New Orleans*. Baltimore: Johns Hopkins University Press, 2009.

Stern, Walter C. *Race and Education in New Orleans: Creating the Segregated City, 1764–1960*. Baton Rouge: Louisiana State University Press, 2018.

Thrasher, Albert. *On to New Orleans! Louisiana's Heroic 1811 Slave Revolt*. New Orleans: Cypress Press, 1995.

Tureaud, Alexander P., Jr., and Rachel L. Emanuel. *A More Noble Cause: A. P. Tureaud and the Struggle for Civil Rights in Louisiana*. Baton Rouge: Louisiana State University Press, 2011.

Turner, Mary, ed. *From Chattel Slaves to Wage Slaves: The Dynamics of Labour Bargaining in the Americas*. Bloomington: Indiana University Press, 1995.

Welke, Barbara Young. *Recasting American Liberty: Gender, Race, Law, and the Railroad Revolution, 1865–1920*. New York: Cambridge University Press, 2001.

Winters, John D. *The Civil War in Louisiana*. Baton Rouge, LA: Louisiana State University Press, 1963.

Woodward, Colin Edward. *Marching Masters: Slavery, Race, and the Confederate Army during the Civil War*. Charlottesville, VA: University of Virginia Press, 2014.

Articles, Reports, Online Features

"The 1619 Project." *New York Times Magazine*, August 18, 2019.

Adelson, Jeff. "A New Orleans commission will review Confederate, white supremacist streets, City Council says." *Nola.com*. June 18, 2020. Available at: https://www.nola.com/news/politics/article_4f65162e-b182-11ea-9696-13f604f4a0ef.html.

Adelson, Jeff, Gordon Russell, and John Simerman. "How an abnormal Louisiana law deprives, discriminates and drives incarceration: Tilting the scales." *The Advocate*, April 1, 2018. Available at: https://www.nola.com/news/courts/article_8e284de1-9c5c-5d77-bcc5-6e22a3053aa0.html.

"Albion Tourgée & the Fight for Civil Rights." *Carolina K-12*, University of North Carolina. Available at: https://civics.sites.unc.edu/files/2012/05/TourgeeFightforCivilRights.pdf.

Alexander, Diane, and Janet Currie. "Is it who you are or where you live? Residential segregation and racial gaps in childhood asthma." *Journal of Health Economics* 55 (September 2017): 186–200.

Bacon-Blood, Littice. "The largest slave revolt in U.S. history is commemorated." *Times-Picayune*, January 4, 2011.

Ball, Edward. "Gone with the Myths." *New York Times*, December 18, 2010.

Barnes, Robert. "Plessy and Ferguson: Descendants of a divisive Supreme Court decision unite." *Washington Post*, June 6, 2011.

Bauer, Shane. "The Origins of Prison Slavery." *Slate*, October 2, 2018. Available at: https://slate.com/news-and-politics/2018/10/origin-prison-slavery-shane-bauer-american-prison-excerpt.html.

Becknell, Clarence A., Thomas Price, Don Short. "History of the Zulu Social Aid & Pleasure Club." Kreweofzulu.com website. Available at: http://www.kreweofzulu.com/history.

"Black History at LSU." Louisiana State University. Available at: https://www.lsu.edu/diversity/aacc/history/lsublackhistoryinfo.php.

Boissoneault, Lorraine. "The Deadliest Massacre in Reconstruction-Era Louisiana Happened 150 Years Ago." *Smithsonian Magazine*, September 28, 2018.

Bordelon, Pam. "New Orleans' preservation efforts honored." *The Advocate*, September 19, 2017.

Bouie, Jamelle. "The Racial Character of Inequality in America." *New York Times*, April 19, 2020.

Brattain, Michelle. "Miscegenation and Competing Definitions of Race in Twentieth-Century Louisiana." *The Journal of Southern History* 71, no. 3 (August 2005): 621–58.

Brenc, Willie. "St. Augustine Catholic Church, New Orleans, Louisiana (1841–)." BlackPast.org. Available at: https://www.blackpast.org/african-american-history/st-augustine-catholic-church-new-orleans-louisiana-1841.

Bridges, Khiara M. "Implicit Bias and Racial Disparities in Health Care." American Bar Association, *Human Rights Magazine* 43, no. 3: The State of Healthcare in the United States (August 2018).

Brown, DeNeen. "The determined father who took Linda Brown by the hand and made history." *Washington Post*, March 27, 2018.

Burch, Audra D.S. "Connected to a President, by Slavery." *New York Times*, July 8, 2019.

Burkes, Caitie. "'Lunch with a Legend' welcomes first African-American LSU student." *Reveille*, April 14, 2015. Available at: https://www.lsureveille.com/daily/lunch-with-a-legend-welcomes-first-african-american-lsu-student/article_d0ac2878-e2ff-11e4-8ee7-37f01c018f9f.html.

"The Cabildo: Two Centuries of Louisiana History." *Louisiana State Museum Online Exhibits*. Available at: https://www.crt.state.la.us/louisiana-state-museum/online-exhibits/the-cabildo/index.

Chamberlain, Charles, and Lo Faber. "Spanish Colonial Louisiana." *64 Parishes*, magazine of the Louisiana Endowment for the Humanities. Available at: https://64parishes.org/entry/spanish-colonial-louisiana.

Cherrie, Lolita V. "A Community Builds a School 1905–1929." CreoleGen website. Available at: http://www.creolegen.org/2013/03/30/a-community-builds-a-school-1905-1929.

———. "History of the Original Illinois Club (1895)." CreoleGen website. Available at: http://www.creolegen.org/2015/02/06/history-of-the-original-illinois-club-1895.

"The Civil Rights Act of 1964." *Teaching Tolerance*, Southern Poverty Law Center. Available at: http://www.tolerance.org/sites/default/files/general/tt_marriage_equality_5.pdf.

"Civil rights legend honored with music, discussion, and a

performance by NOCCA students." *The NOCCA Institute*. Available at: https://noccainstitute.com/2010/05/ monday-june-7-plessy-day.

Clark, Kenneth B., and Mamie P. Clark. "Racial identification and preference among negro children." In E. L. Hartley (ed.), *Readings in Social Psychology*, pages 169–78. New York: Holt, Rinehart, and Winston, 1947.

Cotter, Holland. "John T. Scott, New Orleans Sculptor, Dies at 67." *New York Times*, September 4, 2007.

Daniszewski, John. "The decision to capitalize Black." *The Definitive Source* blog. AP. June 19, 2020.

———. "Why we will lowercase white." *The Definitive Source* blog. AP. July 20, 2020.

Del Sol, Danielle. "Descendants of landmark Plessy v. Ferguson case join forces to further civil rights education." *Preservation Resource Center of New Orleans*. Available at: https://prcno.org/ directors-spotlight-plessy-ferguson.

———. "The Triumphant Return of the Pythian." *Preservation Resource Center of New Orleans*. Available at: https://prcno.org/ triumphant-return-pythian.

"Dred Scott Chronology." *The Revised Dred Scott Case Collection*. Washington University Digital Gateway. Available at: http:// digital.wustl.edu/dredscott/chronology.html.

Dreilinger, Danielle. "The old slaveholder and Confederate names of New Orleans schools." *Times-Picayune*, May 17, 2017.

"The Duplissey Family, August 29, 2004." USGenWeb Archives. Available at: http://files.usgwarchives.net/la/winn/history/ gms6thedupli.txt.

Eligon, John. "After Lynching of Four in 1912, Two Women Come Together as Friends." *New York Times*, May 5, 2018.

Eligon, John, and Audra D.S. Burch. "Reviving Faded Memories of the Violent 'Red Summer' of 1919." *New York Times*, September 1, 2019.

Erqou, Sebhat, Jane E. Clougherty, Oladipupo Olafiranye, Jared W. Magnani, Aryan Aiyer, Sheila Tripathy, Ellen Kinnee, Kevin E. Kip, and Steven E. Reis. "Particulate Matter Air Pollution and Racial Differences in Cardiovascular Disease Risk." *Arteriosclerosis, Thrombosis, and Vascular Biology*, 2018; 38:935–942.

Esker, Fritz. "Section of Press Street to be renamed Homer Plessy Way." *Louisiana Weekly*, April 9, 2018.

Etheridge, Frank. "Derailing Plessy Park." *Gambit*, July 4, 2005. Available at: https://www.theadvocate.com/gambit/new_ orleans/news/article_380f9d31-3eb7-59e1-a4ec-16059a910528. html.

Fessenden, Marissa. "How a Nearly Successful Slave Revolt Was Intentionally Lost to History." *Smithsonian Magazine*, January 8, 2016.

"Figures of Justice Information Sheet." Office of the Curator, Supreme Court of the United States. Available at: https://www.supremecourt.gov/about/figuresofjustice.pdf.

Finch, Susan. "Shared legacy." *Times-Picayune*, May 2, 2007.

Geronimus, Arline T., ScD, Margaret Hicken, MPH, Danya Keene, MAT, and John Bound, PhD. "'Weathering' and Age Patterns of Allostatic Load Scores Among Blacks and Whites in the United States." *American Journal of Public Health*. May 2006; 96(5): 826–33.

Gibson, Charisse. "Heirs of Plessy v. Ferguson team up for change." WWLTV. Available at: https://www.wwltv.com/article/news/local/heirs-of-plessy-v-ferguson-team-up-for-change/289-f42547c7-31c0-4c12-a6fb-113eccoc1db9.

"Governor Edwards Announces Dr. Courtney Phillips as Secretary of the Louisiana Department of Health." Available at: https://gov.louisiana.gov/index.cfm/newsroom/detail/2362.

Greenblatt, Alan. "The Racial History of the 'Grandfather Clause.'" NPR. October 22, 2013. Available at: https://www.npr.org/sections/codeswitch/2013/10/21/239081586/the-racial-history-of-the-grandfather-clause.

Gugliotta, Guy. "New Estimate Raises Civil War Death Toll." *New York Times*, April 2, 2012.

Harter, Christopher. "NOLA4Women: Valena C. Jones' Legacy in Two Cities." Amistad Research Center. April 20, 2017. Available at: https://www.amistadresearchcenter.org/single-post/2017/04/10/NOLA4Women-Valena-C-Jones'-Legacy-in-Two-Cities.

Hartford, Bruce. "Voting Rights: Are you 'Qualified' to Vote? Take a 'Literacy Test' to Find Out." *Civil Rights Movement Archive*. Available at: https://www.crmvet.org/info/lithome.htm.

Henderson, Michael Nolden. "Yes, We Were There at the Battle of New Orleans Jan 8, 1815." Available at: http://findingagnesmathieu.blogspot.com/2012/10/yes-we-were-there-at-battle-of-new.html.

Hill, Ashlee. "School site honored as historic landmark." *Louisiana Weekly*, November 23, 2015. Available at: http://www.louisianaweekly.com/school-site-honored-as-historic-landmark.

"Honored 58 years after integrating LSU." *Louisiana Weekly*, August 1, 2011.

Itkin, Beth Kressel. "Creating 'What Might Have Been a Fuss': The Many Faces of Equal Public Rights in Reconstruction-Era Louisiana." *Louisiana History* 56, no. 1 (2015): 42–74.

Jacobs, Peter. "The Intentionally Confusing Reading Test That Was Given to Black Louisiana Voters in 1964." *Business Insider*, November 13, 2014. Available at: https://www.businessinsider.com/reading-test-given-to-black-louisiana-voters-in-1964-2014-11.

Jan, Tracy. "Racial discrimination in mortgage lending in the 1930s shaped the demographic and wealth patterns of American communities today." *Washington Post*, March 28, 2018.

"Johnson, Bernette Joshua." Amistad Research Center website. Available at: http://amistadresearchcenter.tulane.edu/archon/?p=creators/creator&id=829.

Kennedy, Al. "The History of Public Education in New Orleans Still Matters" (2016). History Faculty Publications, University of New Orleans. Paper 5. Available at: http://scholarworks.uno.edu/hist_facpubs/5.

"Kenneth and Mamie Clark Doll." National Park Service. Available at: https://www.nps.gov/brvb/learn/historyculture/clarkdoll.htm.

Kickler, Troy L. "Albion Tourgée (1838–1905)." *North Carolina History Encyclopedia*. Available at: https://northcarolinahistory.org/encyclopedia/albion-tourgee-1838-1905.

King, Gilbert. "The Great Dissenter and His Half-Brother." *Smithsonian Magazine*, December 20, 2011.

Kinzer, Charles E. "The Band of Music of the First Battalion of Free Men of Color and the Siege of New Orleans, 1814–1815." *American Music* 10, no. 3 (Fall 1992): 348–69.

Lamb, Gregory M. "Descendants team up to teach the positive lessons of the infamous 'Plessy v. Ferguson.'" *Christian Science Monitor*, June 10, 2011.

Landrieu, Mitch. "How I Learned About the 'Cult of the Lost Cause.'" *Smithsonian Magazine*, March 12, 2018.

Larino, Jennifer. "8 Reasons why New Orleans neighborhoods remain segregated." *Times-Picayune*, April 6, 2018.

Layton, Alex. "Angola Prison and the Ethics of Prison Labor." *The Prindle Post*, Janet Prindle Institute for Ethics, DePauw University, January 29, 2019. Available at: https://www.prindlepost.org/2019/01/angola-prison-ethics-prison-labor.

Leah, Heather. "Hidden History: The lost names and stories of Raleigh's enslaved community." WRAL. Available at: https://www.wral.com/hidden-history-the-lost-names-and-stories-of-raleigh-s-enslaved-community/18914528.

Lee, Trymaine. "A Vast Wealth Gap." *New York Times Magazine*, August 18, 2019.

"The Leona Tate Foundation Purchases McDonogh 19 School." *The New Orleans Tribune*. Available at: http://theneworleanstribune.

com/the-leona-tate-foundation-purchases-mcdonogh-19-school.

Leslie, J. Paul. "Compromise of 1877." *64 Parishes*, magazine of the Louisiana Endowment for the Humanities. Available at: https://64parishes.org/entry/compromise-of-1877.

Lewis, Danny. "The 1873 Colfax Massacre Crippled the Reconstruction Era." *Smithsonian Magazine*, April 13, 2016.

Liptak, Adam. "Justices Ban States' Use of Non-Unanimous Verdicts." *New York Times*, April 21, 2020.

Loewen, James W. "Five myths about why the South seceded." *Washington Post*, February 26, 2011.

"The Long Ride." Students at the Center. Available at: https://issuu.com/sacnola/docs/sac_thelongride2.

Lopez, German. "Louisiana votes to eliminate Jim Crow jury law with Amendment 2." *Vox*, November 6, 2018. Available at: https://www.vox.com/policy-and-politics/2018/11/6/18052540/election-results-louisiana-amendment-2-unanimous-jim-crow-jury-law.

"Louisiana Historical Market Program Guidelines." Available at: https://www.crt.state.la.us/tourism/industry-partners.

Lucas, Julian. "Dread Scott's Rebellion." *Vanity Fair*, September 9, 2019.

"Lynching in America: Confronting the Legacy of Racial Terror." *Equal Justice Initiative*. Available at: https://lynchinginamerica.eji.org/report.

Mancini, Matthew J. "Convict Leasing." *64 Parishes*, magazine of the Louisiana Endowment for the Humanities. Available at: https://64parishes.org/entry/convict-leasing.

Martinez, Julia. "For Civil-War Scholars, a Settled Question That Will Never Die: What Caused the War?" *The Chronicle of Higher Education*, October 31, 2017. Available at: https://www.chronicle.com/article/For-Civil-War-Scholars-a/241627.

McQueeney, Kevin, edited by Kathryn O'Dwyer. "Segregation in Palmer Park." *New Orleans Historical*. Available at: https://neworleanshistorical.org/items/show/661.

Medley, Keith Weldon. "The Birth of the Pythian Temple." *The New Orleans Tribune*. Available at: http://www.theneworleanstribune.com/main/the-birth-of-the-pythian-temple.

Menand, Louis. "The Supreme Court Case that Enshrined White Supremacy in Law." *New Yorker*, February 4, 2019.

Michna, Catherine C. "Hearing the Hurricane Coming: Storytelling, Second-Line Knowledges, and the Struggle for Democracy in New Orleans." Boston College University Libraries. Boston College Electronic Thesis or Dissertation, 2011. Available at: http://hdl.handle.net/2345/2753.

———. "Stories at the Center: Story Circles, Educational
Organizing, and Fate of Neighborhood Public Schools in New
Orleans." *American Quarterly* 61, no. 3 (September 2009): 529–55.
Available at: https://muse.jhu.edu/article/317274.

Muhammad, Khalil Gibran. "The sugar that saturates the
American diet has a barbaric history as the 'white gold' that
fueled slavery." *New York Times Magazine*, August 18, 2019.

"New Orleans' desegregation was rooted in the 1960 Dryades St.
boycott." *Louisiana Weekly*, August 5, 2014. Available at: http://
www.louisianaweekly.com/new-orleans-desegregation-was-
rooted-in-the-1960-dryades-st-boycott.

"New Orleans publicly unveiling slave market tour app." *Associated
Press*, September 28, 2018.

Nystrom, Justin A. "Reconstruction." *64 Parishes*, magazine of
the Louisiana Endowment for the Humanities. Available at:
https://64parishes.org/entry/reconstruction.

O'Donoghue, Julia. "Louisiana approves unanimous jury
requirement, scrapping Jim Crow-era law." *Times-Picayune*,
November 7, 2018.

Pasquier, Michael T. "French Colonial Louisiana." *64 Parishes*,
the magazine of the Louisiana Endowment for the
Humanities. Available at: https://64parishes.org/entry/
french-colonial-louisiana.

Paul, Don. "Jerome Smith and His Freedom-Fighting Peers'
Enduring Light." *The New Orleans Tribune*. Available at: http://
theneworleanstribune.com/jerome-smith.

Pitts, Jonathan M. "Civil rights author cheers public launch of new
commission on Maryland's lynching history." *Baltimore Sun*,
September 13, 2019.

———. "Roger Taney, Dred Scott families reconcile 160 years after
infamous Supreme Court decision." *Baltimore Sun*, March 7,
2017.

"Plessy Paints Pride: The Michelangelo of Jones." *Applause*, a
publication of Orleans Parish School Board, vol. 3, no. 9 (March
1980): 1–2.

"Plessy v. Ferguson: A Century Later." *Times-Picayune*, May 18,
1996.

Plyer, Allison, and Lamar Gardare. "The New Orleans Prosperity
Index: Tricentennial Edition. Measuring New Orleans' Progress
toward Prosperity." The Data Center. Available at: https://
www.datacenterresearch.org/topic/new-orleans-prosperity-
index.

Price-Haywood, Eboni G., Jeffrey Burton, Daniel Fort, and
Leonardo Seoane. "Hospitalization and Mortality among Black

Patients and White Patients with Covid-19." *New England Journal of Medicine*, May 27, 2020.

Reckdahl, Katy. "'Heartbreaking' but 'empowering': Re-enactors recall doomed 1811 slave revolt in Louisiana." *Nola.com*, November 9, 2019. Available at: https://www.nola.com/news/article_cbf8b1a8-0347-11ea-9ad3-d75cd7153d1d.html.

———. "'It's hallowed ground': New plaque honors pioneering black-owned newspapers in New Orleans." *Nola.com*, June 16, 2018. Available at: https://www.nola.com/news/article_f85fbc2a-4147-547b-b242-c17651e41fd1.html.

———. "New plaque recalls rich history of 7th Ward elementary school for black children." Special to *The Advocate*, November 20, 2015. Available at: https://www.nola.com/news/education/article_92ee593f-e9f9-5e6c-896f-58acae375967.html.

———. "Plessy and Ferguson unveil plaque today marking their ancestors' actions." *Times-Picayune*, February 11, 2009. Available at: https://www.nola.com/news/article_a11a310a-0f86-54f6-9a34-89372abf0c91.html.

Reckdahl, Katy, and Della Hasselle. "Leona Tate, developers break ground on new civil rights center in old McDonogh 19 building." *Nola.com*, March 9, 2020. Available at: https://www.nola.com/news/article_c9bf8746-6241-11ea-91ec-9f70a64d5993.html.

"Reconstruction in America: Racial Violence after the Civil War, 1865–1876." *Equal Justice Initiative*. Available at: https://eji.org/reports/reconstruction-in-america-overview.

"Reconstruction in New Orleans: Annotated Resource Set." The Historic New Orleans Collection. Available at: https://www.hnoc.org/programs/reconstruction-new-orleans-annotated-resource-set.

Reed, Germaine. "Race Legislation in Louisiana, 1864–1920." *Louisiana History* 6, no. 4 (Fall 1965): 379–92.

Robertson, Campbell. "Report Documents Over 2,000 Lynchings in 12-Year Period after Civil War." *New York Times*, June 17, 2020.

Rojas, Rick. "2 Jurors Voted to Spare Nathaniel Woods's Life. Alabama Executed Him." *New York Times*, March 5, 2020.

Rosgaard, Jessica, and Wallis Watkins. "The History of Louisiana's Non-Unanimous Jury Rule." *Capitol Access*, New Orleans Public Radio. Available at: https://www.wwno.org/post/history-louisianas-non-unanimous-jury-rule.

Roudané, Mark Charles. "The New Orleans Tribune: An Introduction to America's First Black Daily Newspaper." Available at: https://roudanez.com/the-new-orleans-tribune.

Saulny, Susan. "No Cinderella Story, No Ball, No Black Debutante." *New York Times*, March 2, 2006.

Schermerhorn, Calvin. "The Thibodaux Massacre Left 60 African-Americans Dead and Spelled the End of Unionized Farm Labor in the South for Decades." *Smithsonian Magazine*, November 21, 2017.

Scott, Ayo. "'These Are Times': The Legacy of Homer Plessy." Available at: http://ayoscott.com/times-legacy-homer-plessy.

"Se-Pa-Rate." *The NOCCA Institute*. Available at: https://noccainstitute.com/2010/08/se-pa-rate.

Severson, Kim. "Leah Chase, 96, Creole Chef Who Fed Presidents and Freedom Riders, Dies." *New York Times*, June 2, 2019.

Shaik, Fatima. "The 14th Amendment to Black New Orleans." *Civil Discourse: A Blog of the Long Civil War Era*, November 7, 2018.

Shaw, Jonathan. "Air Pollution's Systemic Effects." *Harvard Magazine*, March–April 2020.

Sherman, Mark. "Supreme Court: Criminal juries must be unanimous to convict." *AP News*, April 20, 2020. Available at: https://apnews.com/a4f065037299491913827b7d8eda9023.

"The Significance of 'The Doll Test.'" NAACP Legal Defense Fund. Available at: https://www.naacpldf.org/ldf-celebrates-60th-anniversary-brown-v-board-education/significance-doll-test.

Skates, John Ray. "The Mississippi Constitution of 1890." *Mississippi History Now*, online publication of the Mississippi Historical Society. Available at: http://mshistorynow.mdah.state.ms.us/articles/103/mississippi-constitution-of-1890.

Stafford, Kat, Meghan Hoyer, and Aaron Morrison. "Why are more black people dying from coronavirus? Medical professionals, activists want answers." *Nola.com*, April 18, 2020. Available at: https://www.nola.com/news/coronavirus/article_ea425292-818a-11ea-a06f-3fc0d06522a1.html.

Staples, Brent. "How Italians Became 'White.'" *New York Times*, October 13, 2019.

"*State v. Homer Adolph Plessy*: 125 Years Ago in New Orleans." *The Supreme Court of Louisiana Historical Society*. Available at: http://www.sclahs.org/2017/11/state-v-homer-adolph-plessy-125-years-ago-in-new-orleans.

Stephens, Alexander H. "Cornerstone Speech." *Teaching American History*. Available at: https://teachingamericanhistory.org/library/document/cornerstone-speech.

Stockman, Farah. "Monticello Is Done Avoiding Jefferson's Relationship with Sally Hemings." *New York Times*, June 16, 2018.

Stohr, Greg. "Non-Unanimous Jury Verdicts Draw Review by U.S. Supreme Court." *Bloomberg*, March 18, 2019. Available at: https://www.bloomberg.com/news/articles/2019-03-18/non-unanimous-jury-verdicts-draw-review-by-u-s-supreme-court.

Sutton, Will. "Will Sutton: Say it loud, we're Black and we're proud. A capital B isn't enough." *Nola.com*. July 6, 2020. Available at: https://www.nola.com/opinions/will_sutton/article_507858e6-bf88-11ea-a773-cf80c9a72273.html.

Tadman, Michael. "The Demographic Cost of Sugar: Debates on Slave Societies and Natural Increase in the Americas." *The American Historical Review* 105, no. 5 (December 2000).

Taylor, Jamila. "Racism, Inequality, and Health Care for African Americans." The Century Foundation. December 19, 2019. Available at: https://tcf.org/content/report/racism-inequality-health-care-african-americans/?agreed=1.

Taylor, Michael. "Free People of Color in Louisiana: Revealing an Unknown Past." Louisiana State University Libraries. Available at: https://www.lib.lsu.edu/sites/all/files/sc/fpoc/history.html.

"Valena C. Jones Elementary was a 'sacred space' for children of the 7th Ward." WGNO.com. Available at: https://wgno.com/2018/02/23/valena-c-jones-elementary-was-a-sacred-space-for-children-of-the-7th-ward.

Villarosa, Linda. "Medical Inequality." *New York Times Magazine*, August 18, 2019.

———. "Who Lives? Who Dies?" (online title "A Terrible Price"). *New York Times Magazine*, May 3, 2020.

Vincent, Charles. "Oscar Dunn." *64 Parishes*, magazine of the Louisiana Endowment for the Humanities. Available at: https://64parishes.org/entry/oscar-dunn-2.

"The Voting Rights Act of 1965." *Teaching Tolerance*, Southern Poverty Law Center. Available at: https://www.tolerance.org/sites/default/files/general/voting%20rights%20act.pdf.

Waldman, Katy. "Slave or Enslaved Person?" *Slate*, May 19, 2015. Available at: https://slate.com/human-interest/2015/05/historians-debate-whether-to-use-the-term-slave-or-enslaved-person.html.

Waxman, Olivia. "Years Before Rosa Parks, Sarah Keys Refused to Give Up Her Seat on a Bus. Now She's Being Honored in the City Where She Was Arrested." *TIME.com*. Available at: https://time.com/5871245/sarah-keys-evans.

Wendland, Tegan. "With Lee Statue's Removal, Another Battle of New Orleans Comes to a Close." WWNO—New Orleans Public Radio. Available at: https://www.npr.org/2017/05/20/529232823/with-lee-statues-removal-another-battle-of-new-orleans-comes-to-a-close.

Woodward, Alex. "How 'redlining' shaped New Orleans neighborhoods—is it too late to be fixed?" *Gambit*, January 21,

2019. Available at: https://www.theadvocate.com/gambit/new_
orleans/news/article_e0b3b32e-19e4-11e9-8850-ebd36b3c414d.
html.

Yancy, Clyde W., MD, MSc. "COVID-19 and African Americans."
JAMA, Journal of the American Medical Association, April 15, 2020.

"A Young Boy's Stand on a New Orleans Streetcar." *NPR Morning
Edition*, December 1, 2006. Available at: https://www.npr.org/
templates/story/story.php?storyId=6562915.

Zorn, Eric. "The shift from 'slave' to 'enslaved person' may be
difficult, but it's important." *Chicago Tribune*, September 6, 2019.

Films, Videos, and Apps

13th—a film on the 13th Amendment and the U.S. prison system,
directed by Ava DuVernay. Available on Netflix.

*A More or Less Perfect Union, A Personal Exploration by Judge Douglas
Ginsburg. Episode Three: Our Constitution at Risk*. PBS. Available
at: https://www.pbs.org/wnet/more-less-perfect-union/video/
our-constitution-at-risk.

A House Divided—Documentary and Interviews Collection. New
Orleans: Xavier University of Louisiana Drexel Center, 1987.
Available at: https://cdm16948.contentdm.oclc.org/digital/
collection/p16948coll17/id/0.

History Detectives: Galvez Papers. PBS. Features Michael Nolden
Henderson and some of his findings from his genealogical
research. Available at: https://www.pbs.org/video/history-
detectives-galvez-papers.

Member of the Club, directed by Phoebe Ferguson. Bayou and Me
Productions, 2008.

"#MemorialForUsAll: Flee As a Bird/Oh Didn't He Ramble:
Wynton Marsalis & Friends." Video available at: https://youtube/
Go26TvfhxHM.

New Orleans Slave Trade App. Available at: https://www.
neworleansslavetrade.org.

The Perfect Storm: The Takeover of New Orleans Public Schools,
directed by Phoebe Ferguson and Dr. Raynard Sanders.
Bayou and Me Productions. Available at: https://vimeo.com/
bayouandme.

Plessy Day 2020. Produced by the Plessy and Ferguson
Foundation. Available at: https://www.facebook.com/
PlessyAndFergusonFoundation/videos/313372769653850/.

Systemic Racism Explained. ACT-TV. Available at: https://www.
youtube.com/watch?v=YrHIQIO_bdQ.

Legal Documents

"Additional Amendments to the Constitution." *Bill of Rights Institute*. Available at: https://billofrightsinstitute.org/wp-content/uploads/2019/08/Other.Amendments01.pdf.

"*Barthe v. City of New Orleans, Louisiana*, 219 F. Supp. 788 (E.D. La. 1963)." Available at: https://law.justia.com/cases/federal/district-courts/FSupp/219/788/1438374.

"*Bertonneau v. Board of Directors of City Schools et. al.*" *YesWeScan*. Available at: https://law.resource.org/pub/us/case/reporter/F.Cas/0003.f.cas/0003.f.cas.0294.2.pdf.

"*Brown v. Board of Education*, 347 U.S. 483 (1954) (USSC+)." Transcript. Available at: https://www.ourdocuments.gov/doc.php?flash=false&doc=87&page=transcript.

"*Civil Rights Cases* 109 U.S. 3 (1883)." *Justia Opinion Summary and Annotations*. Available at: https://supreme.justia.com/cases/federal/us/109/3.

"Commerce Clause." *Legal Information Institute*, Cornell Law School. Available at: https://www.law.cornell.edu/wex/Commerce_Clause.

"Confederate States of America—Mississippi Secession: A Declaration of the Immediate Causes which Induce and Justify the Secession of the State of Mississippi from the Federal Union." *The Avalon Project, Documents in Law, History and Diplomacy*. Available at: https://avalon.law.yale.edu/19th_century/csa_missec.asp.

"Constitution adopted by the State Constitutional Convention of the state of Louisiana, March 7, 1868." Article 99, page 14. *Internet Archive*. Available at: https://archive.org/details/constitutionadop1868loui/page/n4/mode/2up.

"Constitution of the state of Louisiana, adopted in convention at the City of New Orleans, the twenty-third day of July, A.D. 1879." Article 148, page 39, and section on "Suffrage and Election," page 45. *Internet Archive*. Available at: https://archive.org/details/constitutionsta00louigoog/page/n5/mode/2up/search/confederate.

"Constitution of the state of Louisiana, adopted in convention at the City of New Orleans, May 12, 1898." *Internet Archive*. Available at: https://archive.org/details/constitutionsta02louigoog/page/n5/mode/2up.

"*Dred Scott v. Sandford*, 60 U.S. 393 (1856)." *Justia*. Available at: https://supreme.justia.com/cases/federal/us/60/393.

"*Hall v. DeCuir*, 95 U.S. 485 (1877)." *Justia Opinion Summary and Annotations*. Available at: https://supreme.justia.com/cases/federal/us/95/485.

"*Heart of Atlanta Motel, Inc. v. United States*, 379 U.S. 241 (1964)." *Justia Opinion Summary and Annotations*. Available at: https://supreme.justia.com/cases/federal/us/379/241.

"Legal brief (typed manuscript), *Plessy v. Ferguson*, Argument of A. W. Tourgée." Chautauqua County Historical Society. Available at: https://cdm16694.contentdm.oclc.org/digital/collection/NYCCH/id/358.

"Lincoln's Second Inaugural Address." Transcript. Available at: https://www.ourdocuments.gov/doc.php?flash=false&doc=38&page=transcript.

"*Louisville, New Orleans & Texas Ry. Co. v. Mississippi*, 133 U.S. 587 (1890)." *Justia Opinion Summary and Annotations*. Available at: https://supreme.justia.com/cases/federal/us/133/587.

"Maryland House Bill 307." (An Act concerning Maryland Truth and Reconciliation Commission). *Legal Scan*. Available at: https://legiscan.com/MD/text/HB307/2019.

"*Plessy v. Ferguson*, 163 U.S. 537 (1896)." *Justia Opinion Summary and Annotations*. Available at: https://supreme.justia.com/cases/federal/us/163/537.

"*State v. Homer Adolph Plessy* Re-enactment CLE." Mock Trial video. Available at: https://www.lasc.org/Education?p=StateVPlessy.

"*Strauder v. West Virginia*, 100 U.S. 303 (1880)." *Oyez*. Available at: https://www.oyez.org/cases/1850-1900/100us303.

"*United States v. Cruikshank*, 92 U.S. 542 (1875)." *Justia Opinion Summary and Annotations*. Available at: https://supreme.justia.com/cases/federal/us/92/542.

SOURCES

Listed below are sources of information presented in each section of a chapter, identified in most cases by the last name of the author of a book or article. If there is no author for an article, report, online feature, or video, the first two words of the item's title are listed. Abbreviations used for certain references are listed below. For direct quotes from people interviewed by the author (see bibliography), nearly all come from those personal interviews, except where indicated. For direct quotes from others, sources are listed separately here for each chapter.

Abbreviations

AA: "Additional Amendments of the Constitution."

A-A New: Adelson, Jeff. "A New Orleans commission will review Confederate . . ."

A-How: Adelson, Jeff. . . . "How an abnormal Louisiana law deprives, discriminates and . . ."

AHD: *A House Divided—Documentary and Interviews Collection.*

APP: *New Orleans Slave Trade* App.

AWT: "Legal brief (typed manuscript), *Plessy v. Ferguson*, Argument of A. W. Tourgée."

BBS: Rev. Brenda B. Square.

Br-vBd: "*Brown v. Board of Education*, 347 U.S. 483 (1954) (USSC+)." Transcript.

BvB: "*Bertonneau v. Board of Directors of City Schools et al.*" *YesWeScan.*

Constitution-1868: "Constitution adopted by the . . . 1868."

Constitution-1879: "Constitution of the . . . 1879."

Constitution-1898: "Constitution of the . . . 1898."

CRA: "The Civil Rights Act of 1964." *Teaching Tolerance*, Southern Poverty Law Center.

D-Black: Daniszewski, John. "The decision to capitalize Black."

D-white: Daniszewski, John. "Why we will lowercase white."

FIG: "Figures of Justice Information Sheet." Office of the Curator, Supreme Court of the United States.

Foner-R: Foner, Eric. *Reconstruction: America's Unfinished Revolution, 1863–1877.*

Foner-S: Foner, Eric. *The Second Founding.*

KP: Keith Plessy.

L-EJI: "Lynching in America: Confronting the Legacy of Racial Terror." *Equal Justice Initiative.*

LHM: "Louisiana Historical Market Program Guidelines."

Medley-Freemen: Medley, Keith Weldon. *We as Freemen: Plessy v. Ferguson.*

Medley-Life: Medley, Keith Weldon. *Black Life in Old New Orleans.*

Medley-Pythian: Medley, Keith Weldon. "The Birth of the Pythian Temple."

Nathan-R: Nathan, Amy. *Round and Round Together.*

P-ACL: "Plessy v. Ferguson: A Century Later." *Times Picayune*, May 18, 1996.

PF: Phoebe Ferguson.

PPP: "Plessy Paints Pride: The Michelangelo of Jones." *Applause*, vol. 3, no. 9 (March 1980): 1–2.

PvF: "*Plessy v. Ferguson*, 163 U.S. 537 (1896)" (Text of the Supreme Court opinion and dissent).

Reckdahl-H: Reckdahl, Katy. "'Heartbreaking' but 'empowering.'"

Reckdahl-It's: Reckdahl, Katy. "'It's hallowed ground': New plaque . . ."

Reckdahl-Leona: Reckdahl, Katy and Della Hasselle. "Leona Tate . . . building."

Reckdahl-New: Reckdahl, Katy. "New plaque recalls rich history of 7th Ward . . ."

Reckdahl-Plessy: Reckdahl, Katy. "Plessy and Ferguson unveil plaque . . ."

R-EJI: "Reconstruction in America: Racial Violence after the Civil War, 1865–1876." *Equal Justice Initiative.*

SvH: "*State v. Homer Adolph Plessy* Re-enactment CLE." Mock Trial video.

Villarosa-M: Villarosa, Linda. "Medical Inequality."

Villarosa-W: Villarosa, Linda. "Who Lives? Who Dies?"

VRA: "The Voting Rights Act of 1965." *Teaching Tolerance*, Southern Poverty Law Center.

WEB: Du Bois, W. E. B. *Black Reconstruction in America: 1860–1880.*
WGNO: "Valena C. Jones School." WGNO.com.

Chapter 1. Ruled Out (pages 2–9)

Based on interviews with Phoebe Ferguson and Keith Plessy

Chapter 2. Keith Plessy's Long-Ago Relative
(pages 10–35)

First section

BOOKS: Medley-Freemen 67–87, 89–109, 116–17.

Rights Denied section

BOOKS: Baker 12–17; Bell 9–14, 35–40, 74–88, 112, 123–27, 222–39; Clark 148; DeVore 40–47; Hall 5–11, 26–74, 86–95, 110–12, 120–34, 142–46, 157–62, 212–36, 318–76; Henderson; Johnson 1–17; Kein 10–30; Luxenberg 92–103; Medley-Freemen 19–24, 34; Nystrom 18–21; Rasmussen; Schafer 45–47, 97–98; Spear 54–68, 230, 250; Stern 14–49; Thrasher 1–85; Turner 134; Woodward. ARTICLES: "1619 Project"; Bacon-Blood; Ball; "The Cabildo . . ."; Chamberlain; Dred Scott Chronology; Fessenden; Gugliotta; Kennedy 6; Loewen; Lucas; Martinez; Muhammad; Nystrom; Plyer; Reckdahl-H; Roudané; Tadman; Taylor, Michael. INTERVIEWS: Greenwald, Henderson. LEGAL: "Lincoln's . . ." OTHER: APP.

New Rights Gained section

BOOKS: Baker 17–42; Bell 78, 222–82; Desdunes 124–27, 132–35; DeVore 50–81; Foner-R 47–50, 62–66, 262–63; Foner-S 150–51; Hollandsworth 1–5, 149–50; Kein 32–41; Kelley 92–93; Lewinson 18, 29, 36–37; Luxenberg 93, 175–89, 274–78, 302–3, 386, 431–32; Medley-Freemen 20–27, 78–82; Nystrom 32–35, 49–50, 54–55, 66–68, 72–81, 85, 96–103, 131–33; Stern 39–49; WEB 68, 154–59, 314, 350, 451–84; Welke 259, 298, 338. ARTICLES: "The Cabildo . . ."; "Free People of . . ."; Henderson; Itkin; Kennedy 7–9; Kinzer; Nystrom; Reed 379–92; Roudané; "Reconstruction in . . ."; Shaik; Taylor, Michael; Vincent. INTERVIEW: Norton. LEGAL: "Constitution-1868"; "Constitution-1879"; *Hall v. DeCuir.*

Rising Up, Together section

BOOKS: Desdunes 138–39; Medley-Freemen 82–86, 170; Nystrom 151–54.

Sliding Downward section

BOOKS: Baker 23–32; Bell 282; DeSantis 51–69; Foner-R 437, 500, 530–31; Gates 26, 35, 134–35; Keith xi–xviii, 82–110; Lane; Lewinson 56, 68, 81, 86; Medley-Freemen 23, 28, 48–52, 96; Nystrom 171–85, 190; Sanders 5. ARTICLES: Boissoneault; "The Cabildo . . ."; Kennedy 8–11; Leslie; Lewis; R-EJl.

Putting on the Brakes section

BOOKS: Gates 28, 35; Foner-R 587–96; Medley-Freemen 28, 31–32, 95–96, 106, 140–43. ARTICLE: Skates.

Sidebars

Words Matter: BOOKS: Baker 13; Bell 76; Hall 157–59, 175, 187–90; Kein xv–xvi, 8–9, 17, 26–27; McWhorter 124; Nathan-R 12. ARTICLES: D-Black; D-white; Sutton; Waldman; Zorn.
War of the Pews: BOOK: LeDoux 175–80. ARTICLE: Brenc.
Secret Plans: BOOKS: Rasmussen; Thrasher 1–85.
Newspapers Led the Way: BOOKS: Bell 224, 228, 252–56; Desdunes 132–35; Luxenberg 392–93; Medley-Freemen 103–9. ARTICLE: Roudané. WEBSITE: Roudanez website.
Irreparable Injury: BOOKS: Baker 27–31, 38; Medley-Freemen 23, 96–97, 106. LEGAL: BvB.

Direct quotes

page 12: "Among the many . . . rights" BOOK: Medley-Freemen 116–17.
page 21: "had no rights . . . bound to respect" ARTICLE: Menand; LEGAL: Dred Scott v. Sandford.
page 22: "Our position . . . slavery" LEGAL: "Confederate States . . ."
page 22: "the immediate cause . . . revolution" ARTICLE: Stephens.
page 22: "destroying the rights of slaveholders" BOOK: Winters 4.
page 23: "equal protection of the laws" LEGAL: AA.
page 25: "very intelligent . . . gallantly" BOOK: Bell 252.
page 26: "A Free Vote . . . Rights" BOOK: Medley-Freemen 106.
page 27: "It was no . . . massacre" BOOK: WEB 465.
page 35: "irreparable injury to . . . color" BOOK: Baker 28.
page 35: "both races are treated . . . schools" LEGAL: BvB.
page 35: "we are respected, our rights protected" BOOK: Medley-Freemen 32.

Photo caption

page 10: ARTICLES: "Civil Rights Legend . . ."; "Se-Pa-Rate."
INTERVIEW: Cooper.

Chapter 3. When a Plessy First Met a Ferguson
(*pages 36–45*)

First section

BOOKS: Baker 34–37; Bell 280–82; Desdunes 140–48; Luxenberg
392–94, 397–98, 410–13; Medley-Freemen 114–37, 170–71.

Building Wide Support section

BOOKS: Luxenberg 162–73, 243–58, 374, 397–98, 408, 410–13, 415;
Medley-Freemen 53–61, 126–37, 139.

The Volunteer section

BOOKS: Baker 36–42; Luxenberg 181–83, 185, 415–17, 420–22,
425–37; Medley-Freemen 17, 26–35, 135–37, 139–47, 152, 156–57,
159.

Sidebar

A Partnership: BOOKS: Luxenberg 411–12, 415, 434–36; Medley-
Freemen 133, 149–58.

Direct quotes

page 37: "We'll make a case . . . of the law" BOOK: Medley-
Freemen 109.
page 38: "We need leaders . . . citizenship" BOOK: Medley-
Freemen 117.
page 40: "defray judicial . . . of the rich" BOOK: Medley-Freemen
126.
page 42: "The fight we . . . heart" BOOK: Medley-Freemen 155–58.
page 43: "equal protection of the laws" LEGAL: AA.
page 44: "Are you . . . Yes" BOOK: Medley-Freemen 142.

Chapter 4. Forever Linked in History (*pages 46–57*)

First section

INTERVIEWS: KP, PF.

The Legal Argument section

BOOKS: Bell 5; Foner-S 160–62; Luxenberg 417–23, 433–41;
Medley-Freemen 37–52, 111, 140–48, 156–83. VIDEO: SvH.

Risky Choice section

> Books: Baker 33–34; Foner-R 530–31, 550–51; Foner-S 148–56, 160–61; Gates 31–34; Keith 131–74; Lane 186–249; Luxenberg 348–86, 434–50, 452–58; Medley-Freemen 114, 149–58, 174–83, 188, 190–98; Nystrom 220–25.

Sidebar

> A Heavy Heart: Books: Luxenberg 448; Medley-Freemen 173–78.
> Join Hands and Hearts: Book: Medley-Freemen 183.

Direct quotes

> page 52: "There is no pretense . . . pleased" Book: Medley-Freemen 163; Legal: SvH.
> page 52: "Should a white . . . color" Legal: SvH.
> pages 52–53: "the object . . . unconstitutional . . . of law" Legal: SvH.
> page 53: "I return South . . . me" Books: Luxenberg 448; Medley-Freemen 177–78.
> page 56: "violation of personal rights" Legal: Louisville.
> page 56: "if we can get . . . comes up" Book: Medley-Freemen 182.
> page 56: "The people of the . . . subjected" Book: Medley-Freemen 157.
> page 57: "The colored man . . . of success" Book: Medley-Freemen 183.

Photo caption

> page 48: Article: Cherrie—"'A Community . . .'"

Chapter 5. Courtroom Showdown (pages 58–67)

First section

> Books: Baker 37–38; Gates 34–37; Luxenberg 421–23, 466–72, 474–83; Medley-Freemen 190–203, 222–23. Article: Shaik.

Solo Dissenter section

> Books: Baker 39–41; Foner-S 152–55, 160–64, 174; Luxenberg 193–213, 346–49, 387, 483–87; Medley-Freemen 203–8.

"Still Believe That We Were Right" section

> Books: Baker 41–42; Desdunes 147; Foner-S 163–64, 174; Luxenberg 489–91, 496; Medley-Freemen 29, 214–18.

Sidebar

Colorblind Justice: Book: Medley-Freemen 199. Article: FIG.

Direct quotes

page 59: "The old citizenship . . . States" Legal: AWT 31; Book: Medley-Freemen 200.

page 60: "How shall a man . . . tell him" Legal: AWT 18.

page 60: "The Statue itself . . . passenger" Legal: AWT 12; Book: Medley-Freemen 201.

page 60: "Justice is pictured . . . color-blind" Legal: AWT; Books: Luxenberg 471; Medley-Freemen 222.

page 61: "was undoubtedly . . . to either" Legal: PvF.

page 61: "the enforced separation . . . upon it" Legal: PvF.

pages 62–63: "to protect the . . . race" Legal: Civil Rights Cases.

page 63: "were welcomed by . . . equal before the law" Legal: PvF.

page 63: "The destinies of the two . . . this day done" Books: Luxenberg 486; Medley-Freemen 204–5; Legal: PvF.

pages 63–64: "peace impossible," "interfere with . . . of American citizens," "In my opinion . . . Scott Case" Legal: PvF.

page 66: "I have nothing . . . to hear" Book: Luxenberg 490.

page 66: "We think it . . . of resignation" Book: Desdunes 147.

page 67: "In the name of . . . cause is sacred" Book: Medley-Freemen 206.

Photo caption

page 58: Article: Scott.

Chapter 6. The Rise and Fall of "Separate-but-Equal"
(pages 68–81)

First section

Books: Baker 46, 140; Bell 281–82; Keith 166, 199n; Medley-Freemen 187–88, 213–14; Medley-Life 241; Murray 170–95. Articles: "1619 Project"; Becknell; "The Cabildo . . ."; Cherrie—"'History of . . ."; Reed 383–85. Video: *A More or Less . . .* Interview: PF.

Guaranteeing Jim Crow a Future section

Books: Baker 46; Bell 281–82; Medley-Freemen 209–14. Articles: Nystrom. Legal: Constitution-1898.

New Jury Rules section

Books: Bauer 120–30, 150, 170; DeSantis 79–154; Mancini 144–52. Articles: A-How; Bauer; Layton; Liptak; Lopez;

Mancini; Nystrom; O'Donoghue; Rojas; Rosgaard; Schermerhorn; Sherman; Stohr. LEGAL: Constitution-1898; Strauder.

Causing Damage to Neighborhoods section

BOOKS: Baker 46; Rothstein 44–48, 60–67, 74–75, 81–82, 97,
106–9, 147, 177–83. ARTICLES: Jan; Larino; Lee; Plyer; Woodward.

Harming Health, Too section

ARTICLES: Alexander; Bridges; Erqou; Geronimus; Shaw; Taylor,
Jamila; Villarosa-M; Villarosa-W; Yancy.

Protest Continued section

BOOKS: Luxenberg 497–99; Medley-Freemen 219–23.

Sidebars

The Original Jim Crow: BOOKS: Gates 148–50; Rice vii–xxxi, 1;
Southern 90–94.
The Grandfather Clause: BOOKS: Baldino 181, 194; Robinson
98–99. ARTICLES: Greenblatt; Hartford; Jacobs. LEGAL: AA.

Direct quotes

page 69: "That a part . . . carry" ARTICLE: Reckdahl-Plessy.
page 69: "The suffering . . . disaster" VIDEO: *A More or Less . . .*
page 71: "$25.37," "$3.49" BOOK: Lewinson 62.
page 73: "White supremacy for . . . constitution" BOOK: Medley-
Freemen 212.
page 75: "ability to read and write . . . dangerous situation"
ARTICLE: Kennedy, its source is *The Daily Picayune* (*Times-
Picayune*), May 10, 1908.
page 76: "except as . . . crime" LEGAL: AA.

Photo caption

page 68: BOOKS: Baker, 46, 140, 280–83, 301; Bell 77; Kelly 92–93;
Medley-Freemen 79–80; Robinson 92. ARTICLE: Reed 384,
387–88.

Chapter 7. Homer Plessy—Vindicated (pages 82–99)

First section

BOOKS: Arsenault 53; Baker 1–13, 43–65, 87, 136–37, 152–55,
173–215, 258–62, 281–99, 301, 305–9, 331–33, 339–43, 363, 410–23;
Medley-Freemen 221–23; Medley-Life 171–75; McWhorter 29–35,
53; Rogers 49–146; Stern 1–13. ARTICLES: "Black History . . .";
Clark 169–78; "Free People of . . ."; Kennedy 16–17; "Kenneth and
Mamie . . ."; "The Significance . . ." LEGAL: Br-vBd.

Sparking Protests section

Books: Arsenault 99, 192, 255, 266–67, 286, 298, 393, 439, 466, 502, 541, 584; Baker 30, 280–83, 301, 326, 375–76; Barnes 108–205; Foner-S 169–76; McWhorter 40–45, 55–65, 91–94, 107, 122; Robinson 13–17, 89–100; Rogers 68–70, 90–91, 94, 112, 115, 124, 129, 143; Rothstein 147, 177–79, 183. Articles: Commerce Clause; CRA; McQueeney; Paul; VRA. Video: AHD.

Jim Crow Lingers On section

Articles: A-A New; "Black history . . ."; Bouie; Burkes; Dreilinger; "Governor Edwards . . ."; "Honored 58 . . ."; "Johnson"; Landrieu; Price-Haywood; Plyer; Stafford; Villarosa-W; Wendland; Yancy. Interviews: KP, PF, Sanders.

A "Reset" section

Interviews: KP, PF.

Sidebars

Dissent's Impact: Book: Medley-Freemen 205.
Personal Protest: Books: Arsenault 466, 541, 584; Robinson 14; Rogers 112, 115, 124, 129, 143; Article: "A young boy's . . ."; Interviews: KP, Smith; Video: AHD. *Note: There are a few versions of Smith's childhood memory; the account in this sidebar combines two versions, the earliest one he gave and one that the author of this book observed. As noted below, some quotes come from an interview Smith did with 6th graders at Martin Luther King, Jr., Charter School on March 18, 2011, that the author of this book observed and that was donated to the oral history collection of the Historic New Orleans Collection in 2019; another quote comes from an account Smith gave in the 1987 Xavier University documentary video "A House Divided." The StoryCorps interview helps establish the date of the event.*
Changing America: Article: Severson.

Direct quotes

page 87: "To separate them . . . be undone" and "denies to Negro children . . . education" Legal: Br-vBd.
page 89: "No opinion buoyed . . . posterity" Book: Medley-Freemen 205; Article: King.
page 92: "Long before I . . . happened" and "slapped me upside . . . them," "Don't stop" Interview: Smith.
page 92: "She grabbed me and hugged me . . . and said she was proud of me" Book: Robinson 14.
page 92: "Jerome Smith was a . . . Rider" Interview: KP.

page 94: "We changed the course . . . chicken" ARTICLE: Severson.

page 95: "discrimination by hotels . . . the Commerce Clause" LEGAL: Heart of Atlanta . . .

Chapter 8. Digging into Family Roots *(pages 100–109)*

First section

> BOOKS: Henderson; Luxenberg 96–98; Medley-Freemen 19–22, 24–27. ARTICLES: P-ACL; PPP; Robertson. INTERVIEWS: Henderson, KP. VIDEOS: #MemorialForUsAll; "History Detectives."

Phoebe's Discovery section

> ARTICLES: Finch; Saulny. INTERVIEW: PF.

Photo caption

> page 100: ARTICLE: P-ACL. INTERVIEW: KP.

Chapter 9. It's Plessy and Ferguson Now *(pages 110–117)*

First section

> BOOKS: MEDLEY-Freemen 111–12; Nystrom 220–25. ARTICLES: Finch; Kennedy 4–5; L-EJl; PPP; R-EJl; Staples. INTERVIEWS: KP, PF.

Changing the Story section

> ARTICLE: Finch; INTERVIEWS: KP, PF.

Sidebar

> Their Time Had Come: BOOKS: Baker 41–42; Desdunes 138–39; Medley-Freemen 86.

Direct quotes

> page 112: "You weren't alive . . . image" ARTICLE: Barnes.
> page 116: "Our foundation . . . Ferguson" VIDEO: *A More or Less* . . .

Chapter 10. Coming Together *(pages 118–135)*

First section

> ARTICLES: Cotter; Etheridge; Michna "Hearing . . ."; Michna "Stories . . ."; Scott. INTERVIEWS: KP, PF, Scott.

More Markers section

>Introduction: INTERVIEWS: KP, PF, BBS.
>Historical Marker: McDonogh 19: INTERVIEWS: KP, PF, Tate, BBS. ARTICLES: "The Leona Tate . . ."; Reckdahl-Leona. WEBSITES: Leona Tate Foundation for Change, Ruby Bridges Foundation.
>Historical Marker: Valena C. Jones: ARTICLES: Harter; Hill; Kennedy 19–20; Reckdahl-New; WGNO. INTERVIEWS: BBS, KP, PF.
>Historical Marker: Pythian Temple Marker: ARTICLES: Del Sol; Medley-Pythian. INTERVIEWS: Bradshaw, PF.
>Historical Marker: Straight University: BOOK: Medley-Freemen 112, 118, 151, 170. INTERVIEWS: KP, PF.

Plessy Day section

>ARTICLES: "Civil Rights Legend . . ."; "The Long Ride"; Michna "Hearing . . ." 161–63; Michna "Stories . . ." 544–47; "Se-Pa-Rate." INTERVIEWS: Cooper, KP, PF, Sanders. VIDEO: *Plessy Day 2020*.

Mock Trials and More section

>ARTICLES: Liptak; Lopez; O'Donoghue; Rosgaard; Sherman; Stohr. INTERVIEWS: KP, PF, Sanders. LEGAL: "State v. Homer . . ." VIDEO: *The Perfect Storm*.

Sidebar

>These Are Times: ARTICLE: Scott. INTERVIEW: Scott.

Direct quotes

>page 123: "This mural celebrates . . . person" ARTICLE: Scott.
>page 125: "came to . . . future" INTERVIEW: BBS.
>page 126: "Racism is a . . . spread it" WEBSITE: Ruby Bridges Foundation.
>page 127: "We consider Jones . . . that school" ARTICLE: WGNO.
>page 129: "the biggest business . . . in the United States" ARTICLE: Medley-Pythian.

Chapter 11. Inspiring Others (pages 136–147)

First section

>ARTICLE: "Se-Pa-Rate." INTERVIEW: Cooper.

Reaching Others section

>ARTICLE: Reckdahl-It's. INTERVIEWS: BBS, Greenwald, Holt, Sanders, KP, PF.

Listening to the Ghosts section

> INTERVIEW: Kokontis.

Beyond New Orleans section

> LEGAL: Br-vBd. ARTICLE: Brown, DeNeen. INTERVIEWS: KP, PF.
> VIDEO: *A More or Less . . .*

Making It Personal section

> INTERVIEWS: Anderson, KP, PF.

Sidebar

> The Fruits of Your Labors: BOOKS: Luxenberg 450; Medley-
> Freemen 178.

Direct quotes

> pages 137–138: "they segregated . . . afterschool," "fostered
> acceptance . . . count," "The process . . . discussing it"
> ARTICLE: "Se-Pa-Rate."
> page 144: "You may not . . . estimate them" BOOKS: Luxenberg
> 450; Medley-Freemen 178.

Photo caption

> page 136: ARTICLES: "Civil Rights Legend . . ."; "Se-Pa-Rate."
> INTERVIEW: Cooper.

Afterword: Others Coming Together
(pages 149–152)

Information sources for the Afterword come mainly from the
websites of the various organizations listed there, in addition to
the sources listed below.

Dred Scott Heritage Foundation: INTERVIEW: Jackson.

Maryland Lynching Truth and Reconciliation Commission: LEGAL:
"Maryland . . ." INTERVIEW: Schwartz.

A Group of African American Citizens: ARTICLE: Waxman.

Joel Lane House Museum: ARTICLE: Leah. INTERVIEWS: Cobb,
Hubbard.

Time Line Footnote *(page 154)*

> BOOK: Medley-Freemen 24. INTERVIEW: Green.

Family Trees *(pages 158–161)*

BOOK: Medley-Freemen 24, 144, 151. INTERVIEWS: Duplissey, Green, Henderson, KP, PF.

Historical Marker How-To Guide *(pages 163–165)*

ARTICLE: LHM. INTERVIEW: PF.

ACKNOWLEDGMENTS

I seem to be attracted to writing about people whose contributions have been overlooked by history, but who helped make the world a better place, while also taking part in something bigger than themselves. So I was intrigued when I saw a news story several years ago about Keith Plessy and Phoebe Ferguson coming together to create a foundation that keeps alive overlooked stories of African American resistance to injustice. A prime example is the resistance story that links them forever in history.

If their two families—once considered polar opposites in civil rights history—can come together, then there is hope for the rest of us. What a great story to share with young people and adults, too, I thought. It not only provides an opportunity to highlight little-known historic episodes, but also shows that reaching across the divides that separate us is possible, encouraging us all to work together to make things better.

I was delighted when Keith and Phoebe reacted positively to the idea of creating a book about the coming together that their foundation illustrates. They have been very generous and open, speaking with me many times to share their experiences with racism and injustice, both as children and as adults. Their wisdom and sensitivity in discussing these issues has helped me understand my own experiences and my responsibilities in how to respond to the seemingly never-ending examples of injustice. I thank them for their courage and their friendship.

I am also grateful to have had a chance to meet Keith Weldon Medley and hear him discuss in person his impressively researched and dramatically written book, *We as Freemen*. He not only brought Keith Plessy and Phoebe Ferguson together, but his book helped them both learn about the significance of the campaign for justice waged by Homer Plessy and the Comité des Citoyens. His book, which I first read more than ten years ago, introduced me to that story, too, and pointed the way for my own research journey. It was such a pleasure to meet him in New Orleans last November at the Words and Music Festival, organized by One Book One New Orleans. Another important part of my research was the opportunity to be present at the unveiling of one of the Plessy and Ferguson Foundation's Historical Markers: the Straight University Marker, installed on Plessy Day 2019.

Michael Nolden Henderson gave an important boost to my research by sharing with me his extensive genealogical findings, which let me learn more about the family connection between Keith and Homer Plessy, and also about their enslaved ancestors. Bobby Duplissey helped me unravel more of the Plessy family's genealogic history. Warm thanks go to them both, and also to the following who are members of the Plessy and Ferguson Foundation board or are supporters of the foundation's work. They graciously shared with me their feelings about the foundation and its impact on them: Noël Anderson, Will Bradshaw, Dr. Erin Greenwald, Dr. Megan Holt, Dr. Kate Kokontis, Dr. Raynard Sanders, Rev. Brenda B. Square, Leona Tate, and A. P. Tureaud, Jr. I'm so glad also to have had a chance to speak with Silas Cooper, who described the creative process for the NOCCA Institute's *Se-Pa-Rate* production; it was wonderful to see another of his students' terrific performances at NOCCA in 2019.

A very special thank you goes to artist Ayo Scott for creating the dramatic mural for Plessy Park and for allowing images from that mural to appear in the book, including on the cover.

Thanks also go to the many people who generously answered my many research questions or helped me obtain the photographs and other images that appear in the book: Connie Zeanah Atkinson, John Ballance, Erin Bradford, Christina Bryant, Dr. Mary Lane Cobb, Silas Cooper, Jillian Cuellar, Nate Emery, Gabrielle Gaspard, Rhea Garen, Heather Green, Robert Gunn, Brian Hammell, Lanie Hubbard, Ann Ibelli, Simon Ingall, Lynne M. Jackson, Judy Jumonville, Liz Jurey, Alan Karchmer, John LaMagna, Elizabeth McMillan, Wes Michaels, Lisa Moore, Francis X. Norton, Jr., Sally Perry, Connie L. Phelps, Sara V. Pic, Richard Read, Mark Roudané, Lori Schexnayder, Fred Schilling, Will Schwartz, Mynesha Spencer, Rebecca Smith, Peter M. Trapolin, A. P. Tureaud, Jr., and Leon Waters.

I also want to thank Seth Osborne for allowing this book to include the special drawing he created as a fifth-grader that shows Keith and Phoebe's faces combined into one image.

Thank you to the members of the Sarah Keys Evans Project Team (described in the Afterword)—Dr. Charles McCollum, Sr., Dr. Ervin Griffin, Sr., Dr. Georgette Kimball, and Ms. Ophelia Gould-Faison—for sharing news of their efforts to honor civil rights trailblazer Sarah Keys Evans. Thanks also for their ongoing work to bring people together.

Helping to spark my interest in New Orleans history are five veterans of the Freedom Rides who were interviewed in March 2011 by sixth graders at the Martin Luther King Jr. Charter School, as part of an author visit I took part in at this New Orleans school: Jerome Smith, Doratha Smith-Simmons, Matt Suarez, Alice Thompson, and Dr. Elliott C. Willard. The accounts that they gave to the students helped me learn more about New Orleans civil rights history; transcripts of their interviews were donated in 2019 to the oral history archives of The Historic New Orleans Collection. Thanks also to Karen Ott, Fatima Shaik, and Dr. Doris Hicks for arranging that author visit and welcoming me warmly to New Orleans.

In addition, this book would not have been possible without the insights and suggestions from the following individuals who served as "critical readers," taking time to read through the manuscript and offer comments. How lucky to have found such careful, thoughtful readers who helped me shape the book: Phoebe Ferguson and Keith Plessy, as well as Professor Leslie M. Harris, Jari Honora, Dr. Kate Kokontis, Sean Martin, Dr. Raynard Sanders, Rev. Brenda B. Square, and A. P. Tureaud, Jr. Additional thanks go to other critical readers who offered encouragement and support: Professor Kristen L. Buras, Dr. Mary Battenfeld, and Judge Douglas H. Ginsburg. Also helping to shape and sharpen the manuscript has been the editorial team at the book's publisher, Paul Dry Books: Julia Sippel, Will Schofield, and Mara Brandsdorfer, as well as Paul Dry himself, who published my earlier book on Baltimore civil rights history, *Round and Round Together*, which also told a tale about bringing people together. I'm so glad Paul saw the value in again encouraging people to come together to try to create a world where all are accepted and treated fairly. There is someone else, of course, without whom this book would never have happened, my husband, Carl. Thank you, Carl, for constant encouragement, gentle editorial advice, love, and support, as well as for your genuine curiosity about the many stories the book tells.

INDEX

AMY NATHAN is an award-winning author of nonfiction books for adults and young people, including an earlier Paul Dry Books selection, *Round and Round Together: Taking a Merry-Go-Round Ride into the Civil Rights Movement* (2011); Abrams Books brought out a picture book version of that volume, co-authored with Sharon Langley, *A Ride to Remember* (2020). A graduate of Harvard with master's degrees from the Harvard Graduate School of Education and Columbia's Teachers College, Nathan's other books for young people include two on women's history for National Geographic, two on music and dance for Holt, books on homework and allowances, and one about civil rights hero Sarah Keys Evans: *Take a Seat—Make a Stand*. She has also written three music-advice books for adults and young people for Oxford University Press. www.AmyNathanBooks.com